SUCCESSPRENEURS

The Comprehensive Guide To Creating Products, Growing And Scaling Your Business And Living The Entrepreneurial Life

Andrew Taylor

Copyright © 2024 By Andrew Taylor

All rights reserved. No part of this publication may be reproduced, distributed, or transmitted in any form or by any means, including photocopying, recording, or other electronic or mechanical methods, without the prior written permission of the publisher, except in the case of brief quotations embodied in critical reviews and certain other noncommercial uses permitted by copyright law.

TABLE OF CONTENTS

Table of Contents 3

Introduction 5

Chapter 1: From Idea to Product 7

    Identifying Market Needs and Opportunities 7

    Brainstorming and Idea Generation 9

    Validating Your Product Concept 12

    Design and Development Process 14

    Prototyping and Iteration 17

    Launching Your Product 21

Chapter 2: Building a Strong Foundation 26

    Establishing Your Business Entity 26

    Crafting a Compelling Brand 29

    Creating a Business Plan 33

    Legal Considerations and Intellectual Property 37

    Setting Up Your Financial Systems 40

    Developing an Online Presence 43

Chapter 3: Growing Your Customer Base 47

    Understanding Your Target Audience 47

    Marketing Strategies for Startups 50

    Leveraging Social Media and Content Marketing 53

    Sales Techniques and Customer Acquisition 56

Building Customer Relationships and Loyalty 59

Data-Driven Marketing and Analytics 62

Chapter 4: Scaling Your Enterprise **65**

Operational Efficiency and Process Improvement 65

Building and Leading a Team 71

Expanding Your Product Line 74

Strategic Partnerships and Alliances 77

International Expansion and New Markets 80

Chapter 5: The Entrepreneurial Lifestyle **84**

Balancing Work and Personal Life 84

Maintaining Health and Wellness 87

Staying Motivated and Overcoming Challenges 91

Continuous Learning and Personal Development 94

Giving Back and Social Responsibility 98

Long-Term Vision and Legacy Building 101

Conclusion **106**

INTRODUCTION

The sun rose over the horizon, casting a golden glow on the bustling city below. A symphony of car horns and footsteps echoed through the streets as the city came alive with dreams and ambitions. In the heart of this vibrant metropolis, amidst the towering skyscrapers and pulsating energy, there was a place where dreams turned into reality – a place where entrepreneurs thrived and the entrepreneurial spirit flourished. This is the story of " Successpreneurs."

Meet Sarah Mitchell, a young and determined woman with a fire burning in her heart. From a young age, she had always been captivated by the idea of creating something from nothing, of building her empire, and leaving a lasting impact on the world. She was not content with the mundane, the ordinary; she yearned for something greater. And so, she set out on a journey to unlock the secrets of success.

Sarah had always been an avid reader, devouring books on business, leadership, and entrepreneurship. But she felt that something was missing. She craved a guide that would take her hand and lead her through the intricate maze of challenges that lay ahead. Thus, the idea for "Successpreneurs" was born – a comprehensive guidebook that would provide aspiring entrepreneurs with the knowledge, tools, and inspiration they needed to create products, grow and scale their enterprises, and live the entrepreneurial dream.

As Sarah delved deeper into the world of entrepreneurship, she realized that the path to success was not a straightforward one. It was fraught with obstacles, setbacks, and moments of self-doubt. But she also discovered that success was not reserved for a select few; it was within reach for anyone willing to put in the work and embrace the entrepreneurial mindset.

"Successpreneurs" would be more than just a book. It would be a companion, a mentor, and a confidant for those embarking on their entrepreneurial journey. It would dive into the nitty-gritty details of product creation, exploring the process of transforming a mere idea into a tangible reality. It would unravel the mysteries of marketing, sales, and customer acquisition, revealing strategies that would help entrepreneurs navigate the ever-evolving landscape of business.

But "Successpreneurs" would go beyond the practical aspects of entrepreneurship. It would explore the mindset of a successful entrepreneur – the resilience, the determination, and the unwavering belief in oneself. It would share stories of triumph and failure, of entrepreneurs who had faced seemingly insurmountable odds and emerged stronger than ever. It would inspire readers to embrace failure as an opportunity for growth, to persevere when the going got tough, and to never lose sight of their dreams.

Sarah's journey to bring "Successpreneurs" to life was not an easy one. She faced countless challenges along the way – from battling self-doubt to navigating the intricacies of publishing. But she persisted, fueled by her unwavering belief in the power of entrepreneurship to change lives. And as she poured her heart and soul into the pages of "Successpreneurs," she knew that she was creating something special – a roadmap for aspiring entrepreneurs to follow, a beacon of hope and guidance in an often-uncertain world.

As the city buzzed with anticipation, Sarah put the finishing touches on "Successpreneurs." The manuscript lay before her, a testament to her determination and unwavering commitment to her vision. She knew that this was just the beginning – the beginning of a journey that would touch the lives of countless individuals, empowering them to pursue their dreams and create a life of purpose and fulfillment.

And so, dear reader, join us on this extraordinary journey as we dive into the world of "Successpreneurs." Let the pages of this comprehensive guide inspire you, guide you, and ignite the fire within you. Within these words lie the secrets to creating products, growing and scaling your enterprise, and living the entrepreneurial dream. Are you ready to embark on this adventure? The path to success awaits.

CHAPTER 1: FROM IDEA TO PRODUCT

Identifying Market Needs and Opportunities

In the journey of transforming an idea into a successful product, one of the crucial steps is identifying market needs and opportunities. This process involves understanding the demands and desires of potential customers, recognizing gaps in the market, and uncovering opportunities for innovation and growth. By conducting thorough market research and analysis, entrepreneurs can gain valuable insights that will shape the development and success of their products.

Market needs assessment is the foundation upon which a successful business is built. It involves delving deep into the target market, comprehending the pain points and desires of potential customers, and identifying the gaps that exist in satisfying their needs. This critical analysis allows entrepreneurs to tailor their products to address these unmet needs, providing solutions that resonate with the target audience.

To embark on this journey of identifying market needs, entrepreneurs must first define their target audience. This involves creating buyer personas or profiles that capture the characteristics, preferences, and behaviors of the ideal customer. By understanding the demographics, psychographics, and motivations of their target audience, entrepreneurs can gain a clearer picture of the needs and desires that drive their purchasing decisions.

Once the target audience is defined, entrepreneurs can conduct comprehensive market research to gather relevant data and insights. This research can take various forms, including surveys, interviews, focus groups, and analysis of existing market data. These approaches help entrepreneurs gather qualitative and quantitative information about customer preferences, market trends, emerging technologies, and competitive landscapes.

Market research also enables entrepreneurs to identify untapped opportunities within the market. By carefully analyzing the data collected, entrepreneurs can uncover niches, underserved segments, or emerging trends that present opportunities for innovation and growth. These insights can guide the development of unique value propositions and differentiate their products from competitors.

In addition to primary research, entrepreneurs can leverage secondary research sources such as industry reports, market studies, and academic publications. These sources provide valuable information about market size, growth projections, consumer behavior, and industry best practices. By staying updated on the latest industry trends and market dynamics, entrepreneurs can make informed decisions and adapt their strategies accordingly.

In the process of identifying market needs and opportunities, entrepreneurs should also pay attention to customer feedback and engage in continuous dialogue with their target audience. This can be done through feedback surveys, online reviews, social media interactions, and customer support channels. By actively listening to customer feedback, entrepreneurs can gain insights into areas for improvement, identify emerging needs, and refine their products to better meet customer expectations.

Furthermore, entrepreneurs should analyze their competitors to understand their positioning, product offerings, and market strategies. This analysis helps identify gaps or areas where the competition falls short in delivering value to customers. By leveraging these insights, entrepreneurs can differentiate their products and create a competitive advantage in the market.

Identifying market needs and opportunities is an ongoing process that requires adaptability and a deep understanding of the target audience. It is not a one-time activity but rather a continuous effort to stay attuned to evolving customer preferences and market dynamics. By embracing a customer-centric mindset and being proactive in seeking opportunities, entrepreneurs can position themselves for success in creating products that truly resonate with their target market.

Identifying market needs and opportunities is a crucial step in the journey of transforming an idea into a successful product. By conducting thorough market research, defining the target audience, analyzing market trends, and actively engaging with customers, entrepreneurs can gain valuable insights that shape the development of their products. This process enables them to create innovative solutions, address unmet needs, and differentiate their products in a competitive marketplace. By understanding and fulfilling the needs of their target audience, entrepreneurs can lay a strong foundation for the growth and scalability of their enterprise, ultimately living the entrepreneurial dream.

Brainstorming and Idea Generation

Brainstorming and idea generation are critical components of the entrepreneurial journey. They form the foundation upon which innovative products and solutions are built. The effective techniques and strategies to unlock creativity, foster ideation, and generate a wide range of ideas that can be transformed into successful products.

1. **Creating an Optimal Environment for Brainstorming**

Brainstorming sessions are most productive when conducted in an environment that encourages creativity and free thinking. To create such an atmosphere, it is important to establish an open and non-judgmental space where all ideas are welcome. Encourage participants to suspend criticism and focus on generating as many ideas as possible, regardless of how unconventional or unrealistic they may initially seem.

2. **Define the Problem or Opportunity**

Before diving into idea generation, it is essential to define the problem or opportunity that the product aims to address. Clearly articulate the challenges, pain points, or unmet needs that exist in the market. This provides a framework for brainstorming and helps participants align their thinking toward generating relevant and impactful ideas.

3. **Divergent Thinking Techniques**

Divergent thinking techniques are effective for generating a large quantity of ideas. These techniques encourage participants to think broadly and explore multiple perspectives. Some popular divergent thinking techniques include:

- ❖ Mind Mapping: Start with a central idea and branch out to related concepts, exploring associations and connections.
- ❖ SCAMPER: Use the SCAMPER method (Substitute, Combine, Adapt, Modify, Put to another use, Eliminate, Reverse) to stimulate creative thinking and generate new ideas by challenging existing assumptions.
- ❖ Random Word Association: Randomly select a word and generate ideas by associating it with the problem or opportunity at hand. This technique helps break patterns and stimulates fresh thinking.
- ❖ Role-Playing and Empathy: Assume different personas or roles related to the problem and generate ideas from those perspectives. This encourages empathy and widens the range of potential solutions.

4. Collaborative Idea Generation

Brainstorming is often most effective when done collaboratively. Encourage diverse participation from team members or external stakeholders who bring different perspectives and expertise to the table. Collaboration can lead to the cross-pollination of ideas, sparking new insights and generating unique solutions.

5. **Idea Evaluation and Selection**

After generating a pool of ideas, it is important to evaluate and select the most promising ones. Consider criteria such as feasibility, market fit, scalability, and alignment with the overall vision of the enterprise. Prioritize ideas based on their potential impact and viability, and eliminate those that do not align with the desired goals.

6. Iterative Refinement

The process of idea generation and refinement is iterative. Once a set of ideas is selected, further exploration and refinement are necessary. This involves conducting market research, validating assumptions, seeking feedback from potential customers, and iterating on the original concepts. Refinement ensures that the chosen ideas evolve into viable product concepts that address market needs effectively.

7. Overcoming Creative Blocks

During brainstorming sessions, participants may encounter creative blocks or feel stuck. In such situations, it can be helpful to incorporate techniques like taking breaks, engaging in physical activity, seeking inspiration from diverse sources, or introducing constraints to stimulate fresh thinking. Encourage participants to embrace a growth mindset and view setbacks as opportunities for learning and improvement.

The brainstorming and idea-generation process is not limited to a single session. It is an ongoing practice that should be nurtured throughout the entrepreneurial journey. Encourage continuous ideation, promote a culture of innovation, and provide platforms for idea sharing and feedback within the organization.

Brainstorming and idea generation are fundamental stages in the process of creating successful products. By creating an optimal environment, defining the problem or opportunity, employing divergent thinking techniques, fostering collaboration, evaluating and selecting ideas, iteratively refining concepts, and overcoming creative blocks, entrepreneurs can unlock their creative potential and generate innovative ideas that have the potential to transform into successful products. Embracing a culture of continuous ideation and innovation sets the stage for entrepreneurial success, enabling entrepreneurs to bring their visions to life and create products that make a meaningful impact in the market.

Validating Your Product Concept

Validating your product concept is a crucial step in the journey of bringing an idea to life. It involves assessing the market demand, confirming that your product solves a real problem or fulfills a genuine need, and ensuring its viability and potential for success.

Before diving into product validation, it is essential to have a clear understanding of your target market. Identify the demographics, preferences, and characteristics of your potential customers. Conduct market research to gain insights into their needs, pain points, and behaviors. This information will be crucial in aligning your product concept with the target market's requirements and expectations. The effective strategies and methodologies for validating your product concept, mitigating risks, and increasing the chances of creating a successful product.

Conducting Market Research

Market research plays a pivotal role in validating your product concept. It helps you gather valuable information about the market, potential competitors, and customer preferences. Different market research techniques can be employed, including surveys, interviews, focus groups, and data analysis. By engaging with potential customers and industry experts, you can gain insights into market demand, identify gaps, and refine your product concept accordingly.

Proof of Concept

Developing a proof of concept (POC) is an effective way to validate the technical feasibility and functionality of your product idea. A POC is a small-scale version or prototype that demonstrates the core features and benefits of your product. By building and testing a POC, you can assess its viability, gather feedback, and make necessary improvements before investing significant resources into full-scale development.

Minimum Viable Product (MVP)

Building a minimum viable product (MVP) is another crucial step in validating your product concept. An MVP is a scaled-down version of your product that includes only the essential features required to address the core problem or need. By releasing an MVP to a select group of early adopters or target customers, you can gather real-world feedback, measure user engagement, and validate the product-market fit. This iterative feedback loop allows you to make informed decisions, refine your product, and enhance its value proposition.

Conducting User Testing and Feedback

User testing and feedback sessions provide valuable insights into the usability, functionality, and overall user experience of your product concept. Engage with a diverse group of potential customers or target users and observe their interactions with the product. Gather feedback on their pain points, suggestions for improvement, and overall satisfaction. This feedback helps you identify areas of improvement, validate assumptions, and make data-driven decisions to enhance your product concept.

Analyzing Competitor Landscape

Analyzing the competitor landscape is an essential component of product concept validation. Study your direct and indirect competitors to understand their offerings, pricing, positioning, and market share. Identify their strengths and weaknesses, and assess how your product concept differentiates itself. This analysis helps you refine your value proposition, identify unique selling points, and position your product effectively in the market.

Iterative Refinement and Validation

Product concept validation is an iterative process that involves continuous refinement and validation. Use the insights gained from market research, user feedback, and competitor analysis to iterate on your product concept. Make necessary adjustments, enhancements, or even pivots based on the data and feedback collected. This iterative approach increases the likelihood of creating a product that truly resonates with the target market and addresses their needs effectively.

Preparing a Go-to-Market Strategy

As you validate your product concept, it is essential to start developing a comprehensive go-to-market strategy. This strategy outlines the steps, channels, and tactics you will utilize to introduce your product to the market successfully. It includes elements such as pricing, distribution channels, marketing campaigns, and customer acquisition strategies. By aligning your go-to-market strategy with the validated product concept, you can create a strong foundation for the successful launch and growth of your product.

Validating your product concept is a critical step in the process of creating a successful product. By understanding the target market, conducting market research, building a proof of concept and minimum viable product, engaging in user testing and feedback sessions, analyzing the competitor landscape, and iteratively refining your product concept, you can increase its chances of success. Validating your product concept helps you mitigate risks, validate assumptions, and ensure that your product fulfills a genuine need in the market. By leveraging data, feedback, and insights, you can refine your product concept and create a product that resonates with your target market, setting the stage for growth, scaling, and living the entrepreneurial dream.

Design and Development Process

The design and development process is a critical phase in transforming your product concept into a tangible and market-ready offering. It involves translating ideas into detailed designs, building prototypes, refining functionality, and preparing the product for production.

The key steps and considerations involved in the design and development process, providing you with insights and strategies to navigate this crucial stage successfully.

1. **Translating Concept into Design**

The first step in the design and development process is translating your product concept into detailed designs. This involves creating sketches, 2D or 3D renderings, and technical specifications that capture the intended appearance, features, and functionality of the product. Collaborate with designers, engineers, and other relevant experts to ensure that the design aligns with your vision and meets the requirements identified during the concept validation phase.

2. Prototyping and Iterative Development

Prototyping plays a vital role in the design and development process. Building physical or digital prototypes allows you to test and validate the functionality, user experience, and feasibility of your design. Start with low-fidelity prototypes to quickly iterate and gather feedback. Gradually progress to higher-fidelity prototypes as you refine the design and address any identified issues. The iterative development approach ensures that your product evolves based on real-world insights and user feedback.

3. Material Selection and Sourcing

During the design and development process, careful consideration must be given to material selection and sourcing. Identify the appropriate materials that align with your product's functional requirements, aesthetics, and manufacturing feasibility. Assess factors such as cost, availability, durability, and environmental impact. Engage with suppliers and manufacturers to source the materials and components required for the production phase. Collaborate with experts to ensure the chosen materials meet quality standards and regulatory requirements.

4. Engineering and Technical Development

Engineering and technical development encompass transforming the design into a functional and manufacturable product. This stage involves detailed engineering, component selection, and ensuring the product meets safety and regulatory standards. Collaborate with engineers and experts to refine the production design, optimize manufacturing processes, and address any technical challenges that may arise during the development phase.

5. **Testing and Quality Assurance**

Thorough testing and quality assurance are crucial to ensure that your product meets the desired standards of performance, reliability, and safety. Conduct various tests, including functionality testing, stress testing, durability testing, and user experience testing. Identify and address any issues or deficiencies that arise during the testing phase. Implement quality control measures to ensure consistency and reliability in the manufacturing process.

6. **Manufacturing and Production**

Once the design and development stages are complete, you can move forward with manufacturing and production. This involves selecting suitable manufacturing methods (e.g., in-house production, outsourcing to contract manufacturers) and setting up the production line. Work closely with manufacturers to ensure smooth production, monitor quality control, and manage production timelines. Consider factors such as cost, scalability, and supply chain management during the manufacturing process.

7. **Intellectual Property Protection**

Throughout the design and development process, it is crucial to protect your intellectual property. Consider filing for patents, trademarks, or copyrights to safeguard your innovative ideas, designs, and technologies. Engage with legal professionals specializing in intellectual property to navigate the complexities of intellectual property protection and ensure your rights are adequately protected.

8. **Continuous Improvement and Iteration**

The design and development process should be viewed as an ongoing journey of continuous improvement and iteration. Collect feedback from users, customers, and stakeholders after the product launch, and use those insights to identify areas for enhancement. Embrace a culture of innovation and iteration, seeking opportunities to introduce new features, improve functionality, and address evolving market demands.

The design and development process is a critical phase in transforming your product concept into a market-ready offering. By translating your concept into detailed designs, building prototypes, selecting appropriate materials, conducting thorough testing, managing the manufacturing process, protecting your intellectual property, and embracing continuous improvement, you can navigate this stage successfully. The design and development process lays the foundation for creating high-quality products that meet customer needs, position your enterprise for growth, and enable you to realize your entrepreneurial dreams.

Prototyping and Iteration

Prototyping and iteration are essential steps in the process of bringing a product to life. Prototypes serve as tangible representations of your product concept, allowing you to test and refine its design, functionality, and user experience. Through iterative development, you continuously improve and enhance the product based on user feedback and real-world insights.

The significance of prototyping and iteration in the product development process and provide practical strategies for effective implementation.

1. **The Purpose of Prototyping**

Prototyping serves multiple purposes in the product development journey. Firstly, it helps you visualize and communicate your product concept to stakeholders, team members, and potential investors. By having a physical or digital prototype, you can showcase the design, features, and functionality of your product in a tangible form, making it easier for others to understand and provide feedback.

Secondly, prototyping allows you to test and validate the technical feasibility and functionality of your product. By building a prototype, you can identify any design flaws, functional limitations, or usability issues early in the development process. This early identification of potential problems saves time and resources by enabling you to make necessary adjustments before moving forward.

Lastly, prototypes serve as tools for gathering user feedback and insights. By putting a tangible product in the hands of users or potential customers, you can observe how they interact with it, understand their preferences, and collect valuable feedback. This feedback guides your decision-making process and helps you refine the product to better meet user needs and expectations.

2. **Types of Prototypes**

Various types of prototypes can be created during the product development process, depending on the specific goals and requirements. Here are a few common types of prototypes:

- ❖ Visual Prototypes: These prototypes focus on the visual appearance and aesthetics of the product. They may include sketches, renderings, or computer-generated images that showcase the product's design and overall look.
- ❖ Proof-of-Concept Prototypes: Proof-of-concept prototypes demonstrate the core functionality and feasibility of your product idea. They are usually basic, low-fidelity prototypes that aim to validate the technical aspects of the concept.
- ❖ Functional Prototypes: Functional prototypes represent a more advanced stage of development. They closely mimic the intended functionality of the final product, allowing you to test specific features and interactions.
- ❖ User Experience (UX) Prototypes: UX prototypes focus on the user experience and interaction design. They aim to simulate the user's journey and provide insights into the product's usability, flow, and overall user satisfaction.

3. **The Iterative Development Process**

Iterative development is a cyclical process of continuously refining and improving your product based on feedback and insights gathered from prototypes and user testing. It involves the following steps:

- ❖ Prototype Creation: Begin by creating an initial prototype that represents your product concept. This prototype should be sufficient to gather feedback and insights from users.
- ❖ User Testing and Feedback: Engage with a diverse group of users or potential customers and observe their interactions with the prototype. Collect feedback on usability, functionality, and overall user experience. This feedback is invaluable for identifying areas of improvement and guiding your next iterations.
- ❖ Analysis and Refinement: Analyze the feedback and data collected during user testing. Identify patterns, pain points, and opportunities for enhancement. Use this analysis to refine the design, functionality, and user experience of your product.
- ❖ Iterative Prototyping: Based on the insights gained from user testing and analysis, create an updated prototype that incorporates the refinements and improvements. Repeat the user testing and feedback process with the new prototype.
- ❖ Repeat and Enhance: Iterate through the prototyping and user testing process multiple times, continuously refining and enhancing the product based on user feedback and evolving requirements. Each iteration brings you closer to a final, market-ready product.

4. **Key Considerations for Prototyping and Iteration**

To make the most of the prototyping and iteration process, keep the following considerations in mind:

- ❖ Clear Objectives: Define clear objectives for each prototype iteration. Focus on specific aspects that need improvement or validation to ensure that each iteration brings you closer to your desired outcome.
- ❖ User-Centric Approach: Place the user at the center of the prototyping and iteration process. Seek feedback from your target audience and incorporate their needs and preferences into the design and functionality of the product.
- ❖ Speed and Efficiency: Aim for rapid prototyping and iteration cycles to minimize development time and maximize learning. Embrace tools and technologies that

facilitate quick and efficient iterations, such as 3D printing, computer-aided design (CAD), and rapid prototyping software.

- ❖ Cross-functional Collaboration: Engage with a diverse team of experts from different disciplines, including design, engineering, marketing, and user experience. This cross-functional collaboration brings diverse perspectives and expertise into the prototyping and iteration process, leading to more well-rounded and successful outcomes.
- ❖ Documentation and Version Control: Maintain proper documentation and version control throughout the prototyping and iteration process. This ensures that you have a clear record of each iteration, including design changes, feedback received, and decisions made. It also helps in tracking the progress of the product development process and facilitates collaboration among team members.
- ❖ Test in Realistic Conditions: Whenever possible, test your prototypes in realistic conditions that closely resemble the intended environment of product usage. This helps in identifying potential challenges, performance issues, or usability problems that may not be evident in controlled testing environments.
- ❖ Balance Innovation and Feasibility: While it's essential to push the boundaries of innovation during the prototyping and iteration process, it's equally important to consider the feasibility of implementing the proposed design and functionality. Strike a balance between innovation and practicality to ensure that your final product is both compelling and achievable.

5. Benefits of Prototyping and Iteration

Prototyping and iteration offer several benefits throughout the product development process:

- ❖ Risk Reduction: By identifying and addressing design flaws, functionality issues, and usability concerns early in the development process, prototyping and iteration help reduce the risk of costly mistakes or failures in later stages.
- ❖ User-Centric Design: The iterative approach allows you to gather user feedback and insights, ensuring that your product is designed around the needs, preferences, and expectations of your target audience.

- ❖ Enhanced Product Quality: Through continuous refinement and improvement, the iterative process helps deliver a higher-quality product that offers superior functionality, usability, and overall user experience.
- ❖ Cost and Time Savings: By catching and resolving design and functionality issues early, prototyping and iteration help save time and resources that would otherwise be spent on rework or redesign during later stages of development.
- ❖ Competitive Advantage: The ability to quickly iterate and enhance your product based on user feedback and market insights gives you a competitive edge by staying responsive to evolving customer needs and preferences.
- ❖ Confidence and Validation: Prototyping and iteration provide a tangible way to validate your product concept, gather evidence of its viability, and build confidence among stakeholders, team members, and investors.

Prototyping and iteration are integral components of the product development process. By creating prototypes to visualize, test, and gather feedback on your product concept, and by embracing an iterative approach to refine and enhance the product based on user insights, you can significantly increase the chances of creating a successful and market-ready product. The prototyping and iteration process empowers you to reduce risks, improve product quality, and deliver a user-centric solution that resonates with your target audience.

Launching Your Product

Launching a product is an exciting and crucial step in the entrepreneurial journey. It marks the transition from product development to introducing your offering to the market and potential customers. A successful product launch requires careful planning, strategic execution, and effective marketing.

The key considerations and actionable steps to help you navigate the process of launching your product and maximize its chances of success.

1. **Preparing for Launch**

Before diving into the launch process, it is essential to lay a solid foundation. Here are some key steps to take in preparation for your product launch:

- ❖ Define Your Target Audience: Identify the specific market segment or customer demographic that your product is designed to serve. Understanding your target audience's needs, preferences, and pain points will help you tailor your launch strategy and messaging accordingly.
- ❖ Competitive Analysis: Conduct a thorough analysis of your competitors' products and market positioning. Identify their strengths, weaknesses, and unique selling propositions. This analysis will guide you in positioning your product effectively and differentiating it from the competition.
- ❖ Develop a Compelling Value Proposition: Clearly articulate the unique value your product brings to the market. Define the key benefits and advantages it offers to customers that set it apart from alternatives. Your value proposition should be concise, memorable, and resonate with your target audience.
- ❖ Set Clear Objectives: Establish specific goals and objectives for your product launch. These may include metrics like sales targets, customer acquisition goals, or brand awareness benchmarks. Clear objectives provide focus and direction throughout the launch process.
- ❖ Create a Launch Plan: Develop a comprehensive launch plan that outlines the timeline, activities, and resources needed for a successful launch. Include key milestones, marketing strategies, communication channels, and launch event details if applicable. A well-structured plan ensures a systematic approach and minimizes the risk of overlooking critical elements.

2. Building Buzz and Awareness

Generating buzz and creating awareness around your product are crucial to build anticipation and generate initial interest. Here are some strategies to consider:

- ❖ Public Relations (PR): Leverage PR channels to secure media coverage, interviews, or product reviews. Craft compelling press releases and media kits to share with relevant journalists, bloggers, and influencers. Highlight the unique aspects of your product and its value proposition to capture attention.
- ❖ Content Marketing: Develop high-quality, informative content that showcases your product and educates your target audience. Create engaging blog posts, articles, videos, or infographics that highlight the benefits, features, and use cases of your product. Distribute this content through your website, social media channels, and guest posting opportunities to attract and engage potential customers.
- ❖ Social Media Marketing: Utilize social media platforms to create a buzz around your product launch. Develop a social media strategy that includes teaser posts, behind-the-scenes footage, sneak peeks, and countdown updates. Engage with your audience, respond to inquiries, and encourage user-generated content to foster a sense of community and anticipation.
- ❖ Influencer Partnerships: Collaborate with influencers or industry experts who have a significant following and influence within your target audience. Seek partnerships for product reviews, endorsements, or sponsored content. Leveraging their credibility and reach can help amplify your product's visibility and generate interest.
- ❖ Email Marketing: Build an email list of interested prospects and potential customers. Develop a series of targeted email campaigns leading up to the launch, providing exclusive updates, early access, or limited-time offers. Craft compelling subject lines and personalized content to drive engagement and conversions.

3. **Crafting Your Messaging**

Effective communication is vital during the product launch phase. Your messaging should clearly articulate the value, benefits, and unique selling points of your product. Consider the following strategies:

- ❖ Unique Selling Proposition (USP): Clearly define and communicate your product's USP. Highlight what makes it different, better, or more valuable compared to existing alternatives. Develop a concise and compelling elevator pitch that captures attention and leaves a memorable impression.
- ❖ Storytelling: Use storytelling techniques to create an emotional connection with your audience. Share the journey, inspiration, or unique aspects of your product's development. Craft a narrative that resonates with your target audience and evokes curiosity and interest.
- ❖ Benefit-Focused Messaging: Emphasize the specific benefits and outcomes that your product delivers to customers. Focus on how it solves their problems, improves their lives, or fulfills their needs. Craft messages that address pain points and demonstrate the value your product provides.
- ❖ Clear and Consistent Branding: Ensure consistent branding across all communication channels and touchpoints. Develop a cohesive visual identity, including logos, color schemes, and typography. Align your messaging with your brand's values, personality, and positioning.
- ❖ Use Customer Testimonials: Leverage positive customer testimonials or early adopter reviews to enhance credibility and build trust. Incorporate these testimonials into your messaging to provide social proof and demonstrate the real-world benefits and satisfaction customers have experienced.

4. **Executing the Launch**

As the launch day approaches, it's important to have a well-executed plan in place. Here are some key steps to consider during the launch phase:

1. Coordinate Logistics: Ensure that all logistical aspects of your product launch are well-coordinated. This includes inventory management, shipping and fulfillment processes, and customer support infrastructure. Be prepared to handle any potential challenges or issues that may arise during the launch.
2. Launch Event: Consider hosting a launch event to generate excitement and create a memorable experience. This could be a physical event, a virtual webinar, or a live stream on social media platforms. Plan engaging activities, product demonstrations, and opportunities for attendees to interact with your product.
3. Monitor and Measure: Implement a system to track and measure the success of your launch. Monitor key metrics such as website traffic, social media engagement, sales conversions, and customer feedback. Analyze the data to gain insights into the effectiveness of your launch strategy and make any necessary adjustments.
4. Customer Support: Be prepared to provide prompt and efficient customer support during and after the launch. Anticipate potential inquiries, concerns, or issues that customers may have and develop a support system to address them promptly. Positive customer experiences during the launch phase can lead to positive word-of-mouth and repeat business.
5. Continuous Marketing: Remember that the product launch is just the beginning of your marketing journey. Develop a post-launch marketing strategy to sustain momentum and drive ongoing sales. Consider implementing tactics such as email marketing campaigns, social media advertising, content creation, and partnerships with complementary brands.

Launching your product is a critical step in the entrepreneurial journey. By following a well-planned approach, building buzz and awareness, crafting compelling messaging, and executing with precision, you can maximize your product's chances of success. Remember to continuously evaluate and adapt your strategies based on customer feedback and market dynamics. A successful product launch sets the stage for growth, scalability, and achieving your entrepreneurial dreams.

CHAPTER 2: BUILDING A STRONG FOUNDATION

Establishing Your Business Entity

Establishing a solid legal foundation for your business is essential for long-term success and protection. Selecting the right business entity is a crucial decision that impacts various aspects of your enterprise, including liability, taxation, and governance. In this section, we will explore the different legal structures available to entrepreneurs and guide them in choosing the most suitable entity for their business.

1. **Understanding Business Entities**

Before delving into the selection process, it's important to understand the various types of business entities:

- Sole Proprietorship: A sole proprietorship is the simplest and most common form of business entity. In this structure, the business is owned and operated by a single individual who is personally responsible for all liabilities and debts. The owner reports business income and expenses on their tax return.
- Partnership: A partnership involves two or more individuals who share ownership and management responsibilities. Partnerships can be general partnerships, where all partners share equal responsibilities and liabilities, or limited partnerships, where one or more partners have limited liability.
- Limited Liability Company (LLC): An LLC is a flexible business structure that combines elements of a corporation and a partnership. It provides limited liability protection to its owners (referred to as members) while offering flexibility in terms of taxation and management. LLCs can have one or multiple members.
- Corporation: A corporation is a separate legal entity from its owners (shareholders). It provides limited liability protection to shareholders, and its operations are governed by a board of directors. Corporations can be classified as C corporations or S corporations, each with different tax implications.

- Cooperative: A cooperative is a business owned and operated by a group of individuals with shared goals and interests. Each member has equal voting rights and shares in the profits and losses of the cooperative.

2. Factors to Consider

When choosing a business entity, several factors should be taken into account:

- Liability Protection: Consider the level of liability protection you desire. Entities like LLCs and corporations provide limited liability, separating personal assets from business debts and obligations. Sole proprietorships and partnerships offer no separation, making personal assets vulnerable to business liabilities.
- Tax Implications: Understand the tax implications associated with each entity type. Different structures have varying tax treatment, including income tax, self-employment tax, and payroll tax. Consult with a tax professional to determine the most advantageous tax structure for your business.
- Management and Control: Evaluate how much control and management flexibility you require. Sole proprietors have complete control, while partnerships distribute management among multiple owners. LLCs and corporations have more formalized structures, with clear guidelines for decision-making and governance.
- Funding and Investment: Consider your plans for raising capital and attracting investors. Certain entities, such as corporations, offer more options for issuing shares of stock and raising funds through equity financing. This may be important if you anticipate the need for significant capital investment.
- Administrative Requirements: Evaluate the administrative responsibilities and compliance requirements associated with each entity type. Some structures, such as corporations, have more extensive reporting and record-keeping obligations, while others, like sole proprietorships, have fewer formalities.
- Long-Term Goals: Take into account your long-term business goals and plans for growth. Consider whether the chosen entity can accommodate future changes, such as additional partners, expansion into new markets, or potential exit strategies.

3. **Seeking Professional Advice**

Choosing the right business entity is a complex decision that requires careful consideration. It is advisable to seek guidance from legal and tax professionals who specialize in business law. They can provide personalized advice based on your specific circumstances, goals, and industry.

4. **Registering Your Business**

Once you have determined the most suitable business entity, you will need to register your business with the appropriate governmental authorities. The specific registration process and requirements may vary depending on your location and the chosen entity type. Generally, the steps involved in registering your business include:

- ❖ Choosing a Business Name: Select a name that is unique, memorable, and aligns with your brand identity. Ensure that the chosen name complies with legal requirements and is available for registration.
- ❖ Filing the Necessary Documents: Prepare and file the required documents with the appropriate government agency. This typically includes filing articles of incorporation or articles of organization, depending on the entity type.
- ❖ Obtaining Business Licenses and Permits: Research and obtain any necessary business licenses and permits required for your industry and location. Compliance with local, state, and federal regulations is crucial to avoid legal issues and penalties.
- ❖ Employer Identification Number (EIN): Obtain an Employer Identification Number (EIN) from the Internal Revenue Service (IRS). This unique identifier is used for tax purposes and is required for hiring employees, opening business bank accounts, and filing tax returns.
- ❖ Fulfilling Ongoing Compliance Requirements: Understand and fulfill the ongoing compliance obligations associated with your chosen entity type. This may include filing annual reports, maintaining proper record-keeping, and adhering to tax obligations.

Establishing the right business entity is a critical step in laying a strong foundation for your entrepreneurial journey. By understanding the different types of business entities, considering important factors such as liability protection, taxation, management, and long-term goals, and seeking professional advice when needed, you can make an informed decision that aligns with your business objectives.

The Choice of business entity is not set in stone and can be reassessed as your enterprise evolves. It is essential to stay informed about any changes in laws and regulations that may impact your chosen entity and adapt accordingly. By proactively managing your legal structure, you can position your business for growth, success, and the realization of your entrepreneurial dreams.

As always, consulting with legal and financial professionals is highly recommended to ensure compliance with relevant laws and to receive personalized advice tailored to your specific circumstances. Armed with the right knowledge and professional guidance, you can establish a sound business entity and embark on a path toward becoming a successful entrepreneur.

Crafting a Compelling Brand

In today's competitive business landscape, creating a compelling brand is crucial for success. A strong brand identity not only differentiates your business from competitors but also resonates with your target audience, fosters customer loyalty, and drives growth.

The key elements and strategies involved in crafting a compelling brand that sets you apart and connects with your customers.

1. **Understanding Branding**

Branding encompasses the various elements that shape how your business is perceived by the public. It goes beyond a logo or a catchy tagline; it encompasses the overall experience, emotions, and associations that people have with your business. Effective branding creates a unique and memorable identity that leaves a lasting impression on your audience.

2. Defining Your Brand Identity

To craft a compelling brand, you must start by defining your brand identity. This involves clarifying your business's purpose, values, personality, and positioning in the market. Consider the following aspects:

- ❖ Purpose: What is the core reason behind your business's existence? Define your mission and the impact you aim to make in the lives of your customers.
- ❖ Values: Identify the principles and values that guide your business. These should align with your target audience's values and resonate with them on a deeper level.
- ❖ Personality: Determine the personality traits that best reflect your brand. Is your brand playful and energetic, or more serious and professional? Define the tone and manner in which you communicate with your audience.
- ❖ Positioning: Analyze your target market and competitors to identify a unique positioning for your brand. Differentiate yourself by highlighting what sets you apart and the value you provide.

3. Researching Your Target Audience

To create a brand that resonates with your customers, it is crucial to understand their needs, preferences, and aspirations. Conduct thorough market research to gain insights into your target audience's demographics, psychographics, and purchasing behaviors. This information will help you tailor your brand messaging and positioning to effectively engage and connect with your audience.

4. Developing a Compelling Brand Story

Crafting a compelling brand story is a powerful way to engage and connect with your audience on an emotional level. Your brand story should communicate your business's journey, values, and the problem you aim to solve for your customers. It should be authentic, relatable, and inspire trust and loyalty. Use storytelling techniques to make your brand narrative memorable and impactful.

5. **Creating a Distinctive Visual Identity**

Visual elements play a significant role in brand recognition and recall. Design a distinctive visual identity that reflects your brand's personality and resonates with your target audience. This includes creating a memorable logo, selecting an appropriate color palette, choosing typography that aligns with your brand's tone, and developing consistent visual assets across all touchpoints.

6. **Crafting Compelling Brand Messaging**

Effective brand messaging conveys your brand's value proposition and resonates with your target audience. Develop clear and concise messaging that communicates the benefits and unique selling points of your products or services. Use language that aligns with your brand personality and appeals to your audience's emotions and aspirations. Consistency in messaging across all communication channels helps build a strong brand presence.

7. **Building Brand Consistency**

Consistency is key to building a strong and recognizable brand. Ensure that all aspects of your brand, including visual identity, messaging, tone of voice, and customer experience, are aligned and consistent across all touchpoints. Consistency builds trust and reinforces your brand's identity in the minds of your customers.

8. **Engaging and Building Relationships with Customers**

Successful brands actively engage with their customers and build strong relationships. Leverage various channels, such as social media, email marketing, content creation, and customer support, to interact with your audience. Encourage feedback, listen to their needs, and provide personalized experiences. Building a community around your brand fosters loyalty and word-of-mouth referrals.

9. Evolving Your Brand Over Time

As your business grows and evolves, your brand may need to adapt to changing market dynamics and customer preferences. Regularly evaluate your brand's performance, gather feedback, and stay attuned to industry trends. Be open to refining and evolving your brand strategy to ensure its relevance and continued resonance with your target audience.

Crafting a compelling brand is a continuous process that requires a deep understanding of your business, target audience, and market dynamics. By defining your brand identity, conducting thorough research, developing a compelling brand story, creating a distinctive visual identity, crafting compelling messaging, ensuring consistency, and actively engaging with your customers, you can build a brand that captures attention, fosters loyalty, and drives business growth.

Remember, a strong brand is more than just aesthetics; it represents the core values, purpose, and promise of your business. Invest time and effort into crafting a brand that authentically reflects who you are and resonates with your audience. With a compelling brand, you can establish a memorable presence in the market, attract loyal customers, and live the entrepreneurial dream of building a thriving and impactful enterprise.

As you embark on the journey of crafting your brand, remember that it is an ongoing process. Continuously monitor and evaluate your brand's performance, adapt to changes in the market, and stay connected with your customers. By maintaining a strong brand presence and consistently delivering on your brand promise, you can establish a reputation that distinguishes your business and fuels your entrepreneurial success.

Seeking feedback from customers, conducting market research, and staying abreast of industry trends are essential practices to ensure that your brand remains relevant and resonates with your target audience. Embrace innovation and be open to refining and evolving your brand strategy as needed to stay ahead in a dynamic and competitive business landscape.

Ultimately, crafting a compelling brand goes beyond creating an attractive logo or catchy tagline. It requires a deep understanding of your business's values, purpose, and unique offering, as well as a genuine connection with your customers. By investing time, thought, and creativity into building your brand, you can create a powerful asset that sets you apart, drives customer loyalty, and propels your entrepreneurial journey to new heights.

The process of building a brand is as much an art as it is a science. Trust your instincts, be true to your vision, and embrace the opportunities that come with building a brand that reflects your entrepreneurial spirit and aspirations. With dedication, passion, and a compelling brand, you can inspire others, make a meaningful impact, and live the entrepreneurial dream.

Creating a Business Plan

In the journey of building a successful enterprise, a well-crafted business plan serves as a roadmap, guiding entrepreneurs through the various stages of business development. A business plan not only provides a clear vision and direction for the company but also serves as a crucial tool for attracting investors, securing financing, and effectively managing resources. In this section, we will explore the key elements and strategies involved in creating a comprehensive business plan for aspiring entrepreneurs.

1. **Defining Your Business Vision and Objectives**

At the core of a business plan lies a clear and compelling vision for your enterprise. Begin by defining your long-term goals, mission statement, and the overarching purpose of your business. Consider what value you aim to provide to your target market and how you envision your enterprise making a positive impact. Clearly articulate your objectives and the milestones you aim to achieve on your entrepreneurial journey.

2. **Conducting Market Research and Analysis**

Before diving into the specifics of your business plan, it is essential to thoroughly understand your target market, industry trends, and competitive landscape. Conduct comprehensive market research to identify your ideal customer profile, assess market size and potential, and gain insights into consumer preferences and needs. Analyze your competitors to identify unique selling points and develop strategies to differentiate your business.

3. **Defining Your Products or Services**

Describe in detail the products or services your business will offer. Outline their features, benefits, and how they fulfill the needs of your target audience. Highlight any unique selling propositions or competitive advantages that set your offerings apart from competitors. Consider pricing strategies, distribution channels, and potential partnerships that will enable you to effectively deliver your products or services to the market.

4. **Creating a Marketing and Sales Strategy**

A comprehensive business plan should include a well-defined marketing and sales strategy. Outline your target market segments and develop strategies to reach and engage them effectively. Define your brand positioning and messaging, as well as the marketing channels and tactics you will utilize to build awareness and drive sales. Include sales projections, pricing strategies, and distribution plans to demonstrate the revenue potential of your business.

5. **Developing an Organizational Structure and Management Plan**

Describe the organizational structure of your business and the key roles and responsibilities within your team. Identify any skill gaps and outline strategies for recruiting and developing talent. Outline the management hierarchy, reporting lines, and decision-making processes. Provide an overview of the legal and regulatory requirements, intellectual property considerations, and any partnerships or external resources that will support your business operations.

6. **Financial Projections and Funding Strategy**

A core component of a business plan is the financial projections and funding strategy. Develop a detailed financial forecast that includes sales projections, costs of goods or services, operating expenses, and anticipated cash flow. Outline your funding requirements and provide a plan for how you will secure the necessary capital, whether through self-funding, loans, investments, or crowdfunding. Include a break-even analysis and demonstrate the profitability and sustainability of your business.

7. **Risk Assessment and Mitigation Strategies**

Identify potential risks and challenges that your business may face and develop strategies to mitigate them. This could include market risks, competitive threats, regulatory changes, or financial uncertainties. Assess the potential impact of each risk and outline contingency plans to minimize disruptions and ensure business continuity. Demonstrating a thorough understanding of risks and proactive measures to address them enhances the credibility of your business plan.

8. **Monitoring and Evaluation**

A business plan is a living document that should be regularly reviewed, monitored, and adjusted as needed. Define key performance indicators (KPIs) and milestones to track the progress of your business. Establish a system for ongoing evaluation and analysis to identify areas for improvement and make informed strategic decisions. Regularly update your business plan to reflect changes in the market, industry, or internal factors.

Creating a business plan is a critical step in the entrepreneurial journey. It provides a structured framework for clarifying your business vision, understanding your target market, and developing strategies for success. A well-crafted business plan serves as a powerful tool for attracting investors, securing financing, and guiding the growth and development of your enterprise.

Remember, a business plan should be comprehensive yet concise, capturing the essence of your business while providing a roadmap for execution. Tailor your plan to the specific needs of your industry, target market, and business model. Seek input and feedback from mentors, advisors, and industry experts to ensure that your plan is robust and aligned with best practices.

Creating a business plan requires a combination of research, analysis, strategic thinking, and creativity. Embrace the process as an opportunity to refine your ideas, identify potential challenges, and develop strategies for success. Be prepared to adapt and adjust your plan as your business evolves and market conditions change.

By investing time and effort into creating a comprehensive business plan, you position yourself for success and demonstrate your commitment to turning your entrepreneurial dream into a reality. With a well-crafted plan in hand, you can confidently navigate the challenges and seize the opportunities that lie ahead on your journey as an entrepreneur.

Remember, the business plan is not merely a document to be filed away. It should serve as a living document that evolves alongside your business. Regularly revisit and update your plan as you gain new insights, achieve milestones, and adapt to market dynamics. Stay agile and open to feedback, continuously refining your strategies and adjusting your course as needed.

Creating a business plan is a valuable exercise that requires careful thought and analysis. It helps you gain clarity on your business concept, identify potential obstacles, and develop strategies to overcome them. With a well-crafted business plan, you can approach investors, lenders, and stakeholders with confidence, demonstrating your preparedness and vision for success.

As you embark on the journey of creating your business plan, keep in mind that it is a tool to guide and inspire you. Embrace the process of exploring your business idea, researching your market, and developing strategies to achieve your goals. With a solid business plan in place, you can navigate the challenges and uncertainties of entrepreneurship with clarity, purpose, and resilience.

Remember, the success of your business ultimately depends on your execution and the relationships you build along the way. A business plan is a roadmap, but it is you, as an entrepreneur, who brings it to life through your passion, determination, and unwavering commitment to your entrepreneurial dream.

May your business plan serve as a compass, guiding you toward your desired destination, and may your journey as an entrepreneur be filled with growth, fulfillment, and the realization of your entrepreneurial aspirations.

Legal Considerations and Intellectual Property

In the dynamic and ever-evolving landscape of entrepreneurship, understanding legal considerations and intellectual property is of paramount importance. As an aspiring entrepreneur, it is crucial to navigate the legal framework that governs business operations, protect your intellectual property assets, and ensure compliance with relevant laws and regulations. The key legal considerations and intellectual property strategies that will empower you to protect your business and foster its long-term growth and success.

1. **Choosing the Right Legal Structure**

Selecting the appropriate legal structure for your enterprise is a critical decision that impacts various aspects of your business, including liability, taxation, and governance. Common legal structures include sole proprietorships, partnerships, limited liability companies (LLCs), and corporations. Each structure has its advantages and disadvantages, so it is essential to consult with legal professionals to determine the most suitable option for your specific needs and goals.

2. **Registering Your Business**

Once you have determined the legal structure, you will need to register your business with the appropriate government authorities. This process typically involves obtaining the necessary licenses and permits, registering your business name, and complying with local, state, and federal regulations. Registering your business not only establishes its legal existence but also enables you to access various benefits and protections under the law.

3. **Contracts and Agreements**

Contracts and agreements play a pivotal role in defining and protecting business relationships. Whether it's a partnership agreement, employment contract, vendor agreement, or customer contract, it is crucial to have written agreements in place to clearly outline the rights and obligations of all parties involved. Working with legal professionals to draft and review contracts can help safeguard your interests and minimize the risk of disputes or legal complications.

4. **Intellectual Property Protection**

Intellectual property (IP) is a valuable asset for entrepreneurs, encompassing creations of the mind such as inventions, trademarks, copyrights, and trade secrets. Protecting your IP is essential to prevent unauthorized use or infringement by competitors and to maintain a competitive edge in the market. Consider consulting with an intellectual property attorney to identify and secure appropriate protections for your unique creations.

- Trademarks: Trademarks are symbols, names, logos, or phrases that distinguish your products or services from others in the marketplace. Registering a trademark provides legal protection and prevents others from using similar marks that may confuse consumers. Conducting a comprehensive trademark search and working with a trademark attorney can help ensure the availability and registration of your desired mark.
- Copyrights: Copyright protection safeguards original works of authorship, such as literary, artistic, or musical creations. Registering your copyright provides legal evidence of ownership and grants you exclusive rights to reproduce, distribute, and publicly display your work. It is advisable to consult with a copyright attorney to understand the scope of copyright protection and navigate the registration process.
- Patents: If you have invented a novel and non-obvious product, process, or technology, obtaining a patent can provide exclusive rights to your invention for a limited period. Patents safeguard your inventions from being used, manufactured, or sold by others without your permission. Given the complexity of the patent process, seeking guidance from a patent attorney is highly recommended.

- ❖ Trade Secrets: Trade secrets refer to confidential business information that gives your enterprise a competitive advantage. Examples include proprietary formulas, manufacturing processes, customer lists, and marketing strategies. Protecting trade secrets involves implementing security measures, such as non-disclosure agreements (NDAs), restricted access, and internal policies to maintain confidentiality.

5. **Privacy and Data Protection**

In an increasingly digital world, privacy and data protection have become critical concerns for entrepreneurs. It is essential to understand and comply with applicable data protection laws and regulations, such as the General Data Protection Regulation (GDPR) and the California Consumer Privacy Act (CCPA). Implementing robust data protection measures, including secure storage, data encryption, and privacy policies, helps safeguard sensitive information and build trust with customers.

6. **Employment and Labor Laws**

As your enterprise grows, it is crucial to comply with employment and labor laws to protect your employees' rights and avoid legal disputes. Familiarize yourself with laws regarding minimum wage, working hours, overtime pay, employee benefits, anti-discrimination, and workplace safety. Consult with legal professionals or labor law specialists to ensure compliance with local and federal regulations.

7. **Compliance with Regulatory Requirements**

Many industries are subject to specific regulations and compliance requirements. Depending on your business activities, you may need to obtain permits, licenses, or certifications. Examples include food handling permits, environmental permits, professional licenses, and financial regulations. Research and understand the regulatory landscape applicable to your industry to ensure compliance and avoid potential legal consequences.

Legal considerations and intellectual property protection are integral components of building a successful enterprise. By understanding and navigating the legal framework, you can protect your business, mitigate risks, and foster innovation. Engaging legal professionals, such as attorneys specializing in business law or intellectual property, can provide invaluable guidance and ensure compliance with relevant laws and regulations.

Remember that the information provided in this section is a general overview and should not be considered legal advice. It is always recommended to consult with legal professionals who specialize in business law or intellectual property to address your specific circumstances and requirements. By prioritizing legal considerations and protecting your intellectual property, you can establish a solid foundation for your entrepreneurial journey, ensuring the long-term growth and prosperity of your enterprise.

Setting Up Your Financial Systems

Effective financial management is a cornerstone of entrepreneurial success. As an entrepreneur, establishing robust financial systems is crucial for monitoring your business's financial health, making informed decisions, and achieving long-term growth. The essential steps of setting up your financial systems, include accounting practices, budgeting, cash flow management, and financial reporting. By implementing these strategies, you can gain control over your finances and pave the way for a thriving enterprise.

1. **Accounting Practices**

Sound accounting practices are vital for organizing and tracking your business's financial transactions. Consider the following key aspects:

- ❖ Bookkeeping: Maintain accurate records of income, expenses, assets, and liabilities. Utilize accounting software or engage professional bookkeepers to streamline this process.
- ❖ Chart of Accounts: Develop a chart of accounts that categorizes your financial transactions into specific accounts (e.g., sales, expenses, assets) for easier tracking and reporting.
- ❖ Accrual vs. Cash Basis Accounting: Determine whether to use accrual or cash basis accounting. Accrual accounting records income and expenses

when they are earned or incurred, while cash-based accounting records them when cash is received or paid.

- ❖ Financial Statements: Learn to prepare and interpret financial statements, including the income statement, balance sheet, and cash flow statement. These statements provide a snapshot of your business's financial performance and position.

2. **Budgeting**

Creating a budget allows you to plan and allocate financial resources effectively. Consider the following steps:

- ❖ Revenue Forecasting: Estimate your expected revenue based on market research, historical data, and sales projections. This will serve as the foundation for your budget.
- ❖ Expense Analysis: Identify and categorize your expenses, including fixed costs (e.g., rent, utilities) and variable costs (e.g., marketing, inventory). Analyze past expenses to make accurate projections.
- ❖ Setting Financial Goals: Define short-term and long-term financial goals for your business. These goals will guide your budgeting process and provide benchmarks for measuring success.
- ❖ Monitoring and Adjusting: Regularly monitor your actual financial performance against your budgeted figures. Adjust your budget as necessary to address changes in the business environment or unexpected circumstances.

3. **Cash Flow Management**

Maintaining healthy cash flow is essential for business sustainability. Consider the following strategies:

- ❖ Cash Flow Forecasting: Project your future cash inflows and outflows to anticipate potential cash shortages or surpluses. This allows you to take proactive measures to manage your cash flow effectively.

- ❖ Managing Receivables: Implement efficient invoicing and collection practices to ensure timely payment from customers. Consider offering incentives for early payments or establishing clear credit terms.
- ❖ Controlling Payables: Negotiate favorable payment terms with suppliers and vendors. Prioritize payments based on their due dates and available cash flow to avoid late fees or strained relationships.
- ❖ Emergency Funds: Set aside a reserve fund to address unforeseen expenses or temporary cash flow gaps. This provides a safety net during challenging times and reduces reliance on external financing.

4. Financial Reporting

Regular financial reporting provides valuable insights into your business's performance and facilitates informed decision-making. Consider the following elements:

- ❖ Key Performance Indicators (KPIs): Identify and track KPIs that align with your business objectives. Examples include revenue growth, gross profit margin, customer acquisition cost, and return on investment (ROI).
- ❖ Financial Ratios: Calculate and monitor financial ratios to assess your business's financial health and performance. Examples include liquidity ratios, profitability ratios, and efficiency ratios.
- ❖ Management Reports: Generate periodic management reports that summarize your financial results, key metrics, and trends. These reports help you evaluate progress toward your goals and identify areas for improvement.
- ❖ Investor Relations: If seeking external investment, prepare investor-focused financial reports, including financial forecasts, valuation analysis, and return on investment projections. These reports demonstrate your business's potential to investors.

Setting up robust financial systems is essential for entrepreneurs seeking to build a solid financial foundation. By implementing effective accounting practices, creating budgets, managing cash flow, and generating comprehensive financial reports, you gain a clear understanding of your business's financial performance and can make informed decisions to support its growth and sustainability.

Remember that the information provided in this section is a general overview and should not be considered financial or accounting advice. It is recommended to consult with accounting professionals or financial advisors to address your specific circumstances and requirements. With well-established financial systems in place, you can navigate the financial complexities of entrepreneurship with confidence and work towards achieving your entrepreneurial dreams.

Developing an Online Presence

In today's digital age, establishing a strong online presence is essential for entrepreneurs to reach a wider audience, build brand awareness, and drive business growth. Developing an effective online presence involves leveraging various digital platforms and strategies to connect with your target market, engage customers, and establish credibility. The key steps of developing an online presence, include creating a website, utilizing social media, optimizing for search engines, and implementing online marketing techniques. By harnessing the power of the internet, you can position your enterprise for success in the digital marketplace.

1. Creating a Website

A website serves as the foundation of your online presence, providing a central hub for customers to learn about your business, products, and services. Consider the following aspects:

- ❖ Domain Name: Choose a memorable and relevant domain name that reflects your brand and is easy to remember and spell.
- ❖ User-Friendly Design: Create a visually appealing and user-friendly website design that is responsive across devices (e.g., desktop, mobile) and optimized for fast loading speeds.

- ❖ Compelling Content: Craft engaging and informative content that showcases your expertise, addresses customer pain points and highlights the unique value your business offers.
- ❖ Clear Call-to-Action: Incorporate clear and prominent calls-to-action (CTAs) throughout your website to guide visitors towards desired actions, such as making a purchase, subscribing to a newsletter, or contacting you.

2. **Utilizing Social Media**

Social media platforms provide valuable opportunities to connect with your target audience, foster brand loyalty, and drive website traffic. Consider the following strategies:

- ❖ Platform Selection: Identify the social media platforms that align with your target audience and business objectives. Examples include Facebook, Instagram, Twitter, LinkedIn, and YouTube.
- ❖ Content Strategy: Develop a content strategy that resonates with your audience and aligns with your brand voice. Create and share engaging content, such as articles, videos, images, and infographics, that provides value and encourages interaction.
- ❖ Community Engagement: Actively engage with your social media followers by responding to comments, messages, and mentions. Encourage user-generated content, run contests or giveaways, and foster a sense of community around your brand.
- ❖ Paid Advertising: Consider utilizing paid advertising options offered by social media platforms to expand your reach, target specific demographics, and drive traffic to your website or landing pages.

3. **Optimizing for Search Engines**

Search engine optimization (SEO) helps improve your website's visibility and organic search rankings. Consider the following techniques:

- ❖ Keyword Research: Identify relevant keywords and phrases that your target audience is likely to search for. Incorporate these keywords naturally into your website's content, meta tags, headings, and URLs.
- ❖ On-Page Optimization: Optimize your website's structure and content to enhance its search engine friendliness. This includes optimizing page titles, meta descriptions, image alt tags, and internal linking.
- ❖ Quality Content Creation: Create high-quality, original content that provides value to your audience. Regularly publish blog posts, articles, and other informative resources that address customer needs and establish your expertise.
- ❖ Link Building: Seek opportunities to build high-quality backlinks from reputable websites. This can be done through guest blogging, partnerships, influencer collaborations, or engaging in industry-specific forums or communities.

4. Implementing Online Marketing Techniques

Online marketing encompasses various strategies and tactics to promote your business and attract customers. Consider the following techniques:

- ❖ Email Marketing: Build an email list and leverage email marketing campaigns to nurture leads, engage customers, and drive repeat business. Provide valuable content, exclusive offers, and personalized recommendations to your subscribers.
- ❖ Pay-Per-Click Advertising: Utilize pay-per-click (PPC) advertising platforms, such as Google Ads or social media advertising, to target specific keywords, demographics, or interests. Set a budget and optimize your campaigns for maximum ROI.
- ❖ Content Marketing: Develop a content marketing strategy that focuses on creating and distributing valuable, relevant, and consistent content to attract and retain a clearly defined audience. This can include blog posts, videos, podcasts, and downloadable resources.
- ❖ Influencer Marketing: Collaborate with influencers or industry experts who have a significant following and influence over your target audience. Partnering with them can help expand your reach and build trust with their followers.

Developing a compelling online presence is crucial for entrepreneurs to thrive in the digital landscape. By creating an engaging website, utilizing social media effectively, optimizing for search engines, and implementing online marketing techniques, you can establish a strong online brand presence, attract customers, and drive business growth.

Remember that the information provided in this section is a general overview and should not be considered professional advice. It is recommended to conduct further research and consult with digital marketing professionals to tailor these strategies to your specific business needs and goals. With a well-developed online presence, you can position yourself as an authority in your industry, expand your reach, and ultimately achieve your entrepreneurial dreams in the digital realm.

CHAPTER 3: GROWING YOUR CUSTOMER BASE

Understanding Your Target Audience

One of the critical elements of entrepreneurial success is having a deep understanding of your target audience. To effectively create products, grow your enterprise, and achieve your entrepreneurial dreams, you must know who your customers are, what they want, and how to engage and serve them. The process of understanding your target audience, includes market research, creating buyer personas, analyzing customer behavior, and leveraging customer feedback. By gaining insights into your target audience, you can tailor your offerings, marketing strategies, and customer experiences to meet their needs and preferences.

1. **Market Research**

Market research is the foundation of understanding your target audience. It involves gathering and analyzing relevant data to identify market trends, customer preferences, and competitive landscapes. Consider the following steps:

- ❖ Identify Research Objectives: Clearly define the goals and objectives of your market research. Determine what specific information you need to gather to better understand your target audience.
- ❖ Conduct Surveys and Interviews: Develop surveys or interview questions to gather insights directly from your target audience. Ask about their needs, preferences, buying behaviors, and pain points.
- ❖ Explore Competitor Analysis: Study your competitors to identify their target audience, unique selling propositions, and marketing strategies. Analyze their strengths, weaknesses, and opportunities to differentiate your offerings.
- ❖ Analyze Industry Trends: Stay abreast of industry trends, technological advancements, and market dynamics that may impact your target audience's behavior and preferences.

2. Creating Buyer Personas

Building buyer personas is a powerful tool to understand your target audience at a more personal level. Buyer personas are fictional representations of your ideal customers. Consider the following steps:

- ❖ Demographic Information: Define the demographic characteristics of your target audience, such as age, gender, location, income level, education, and occupation.
- ❖ Psychographic Insights: Dive into the psychographic aspects of your target audience, including their values, interests, hobbies, lifestyle choices, aspirations, and pain points.
- ❖ Behavioral Patterns: Identify the behavioral patterns of your target audience, such as their buying habits, preferred communication channels, media consumption, and decision-making processes.
- ❖ Needs and Goals: Understand the needs, goals, and challenges of your target audience. Determine how your products or services can address their pain points and help them achieve their objectives.

3. Analyzing Customer Behavior

Analyzing customer behavior provides valuable insights into how your target audience interacts with your offerings and brand. Consider the following strategies:

- ❖ Website Analytics: Utilize web analytics tools to track and analyze customer behavior on your website. Monitor metrics like page views, bounce rates, time spent on site, and conversion rates to identify patterns and make data-driven decisions.
- ❖ Social Media Insights: Leverage social media analytics to understand how your target audience engages with your social media profiles, content, and campaigns. Analyze metrics like reach, engagement, click-through rates, and follower demographics.
- ❖ Customer Journey Mapping: Map out the entire customer journey, from awareness to purchase and beyond. Identify touchpoints, pain points, and opportunities for improving the customer experience and increasing customer loyalty.

- ❖ Purchase Data Analysis: Analyze customer purchase data to identify patterns, product preferences, and buying behaviors. This information can guide product development, pricing strategies, and marketing campaigns.

4. **Leveraging Customer Feedback**

Customer feedback is a valuable resource for understanding your target audience's satisfaction, preferences, and areas for improvement. Consider the following approaches:

- ❖ Surveys and Feedback Forms: Collect feedback through surveys, feedback forms, or post-purchase follow-ups. Ask customers to rate their experience, provide suggestions, and share their thoughts on your products and services.
- ❖ Social Listening: Monitor social media platforms, review sites, and online communities to gather insights from customer conversations. Pay attention to both positive and negative feedback to identify areas of strength and areas that need improvement.
- ❖ Customer Support Interactions: Engage with your customers through customer support interactions. Analyze common inquiries, complaints, and suggestions to identify recurring issues or opportunities for enhancing customer satisfaction.
- ❖ User Testing and Focus Groups: Conduct user testing sessions or organize focus groups to gain direct feedback on new products, features, or user experiences. This can provide valuable insights into your target audience's preferences and expectations.

Understanding your target audience is essential for entrepreneurs who aim to create products, grow their enterprises, and achieve their entrepreneurial dreams. By conducting market research, creating buyer personas, analyzing customer behavior, and leveraging customer feedback, you can gain deep insights into your target audience's needs, preferences, and behaviors. Armed with this knowledge, you can tailor your offerings, marketing strategies, and customer experiences to effectively serve your target audience and drive business growth.

Remember that the information provided in this section is a general overview and should not be considered professional advice. It is recommended to conduct further research and consult with market research professionals to customize these strategies to your specific business needs and goals. By truly understanding your target audience, you can establish meaningful connections, deliver exceptional value, and position yourself for long-term success as an entrepreneur.

Marketing Strategies for Startups

For startups, effective marketing strategies are essential to gain visibility, attract customers, and establish a strong foothold in the market. Some various marketing strategies and tactics are specifically tailored for startups. From creating a compelling brand identity to leveraging digital marketing channels and optimizing customer acquisition, these strategies will help you effectively promote your startup and achieve your entrepreneurial dreams. By implementing these marketing strategies, you can create awareness, drive customer engagement, and position your startup for growth and success.

1. **Defining Your Brand Identity**

Developing a strong brand identity is crucial for startups to differentiate themselves in a competitive market. Consider the following steps:

- ❖ Brand Purpose and Values: Define the purpose and values that drive your startup. Identify the unique value proposition that sets you apart from competitors and resonates with your target audience.
- ❖ Brand Messaging: Craft a compelling brand message that communicates what your startup stands for and the benefits it offers to customers. Ensure consistency in messaging across all marketing channels.
- ❖ Visual Branding: Create a visually appealing and consistent brand identity, including a logo, color palette, typography, and visual elements that reflect your brand's personality and values.
- ❖ Brand Voice: Develop a distinct brand voice that aligns with your target audience and conveys your startup's personality. Whether it's professional, playful, or authoritative, maintain consistency in tone and language across all communication channels.

2. **Leveraging Digital Marketing Channels**

Digital marketing channels provide cost-effective and highly targeted opportunities for startups to reach their audience. Consider the following strategies:

- Content Marketing: Create valuable and engaging content that educates, entertains, or solves problems for your target audience. Publish blog posts, articles, videos, or podcasts that establish your startup as a trusted resource in your industry.
- Social Media Marketing: Identify the social media platforms where your target audience is most active. Develop a social media strategy that includes regular posting, community engagement, and paid advertising to increase brand visibility and drive website traffic.
- Email Marketing: Build an email list and implement email marketing campaigns to nurture leads, promote new products or services, and drive conversions. Personalize your emails and provide exclusive content or offers to increase engagement and customer loyalty.
- Influencer Marketing: Collaborate with influencers or industry experts who have a significant following and influence over your target audience. Partnering with them can help amplify your brand's reach and build trust with their followers.

3. **Implementing Customer Acquisition Strategies**

Acquiring customers is a top priority for startups. Consider the following customer acquisition strategies:

- Search Engine Optimization (SEO): Optimize your website and content to improve organic visibility in search engine results. Conduct keyword research, optimize meta tags and headings, and create high-quality content that aligns with your target audience's search intent.
- Pay-Per-Click (PPC) Advertising: Utilize PPC advertising platforms like Google Ads or social media advertising to target specific keywords, demographics, or interests. Set a budget, monitor performance, and refine your campaigns to maximize return on investment.

- ❖ Referral Programs: Encourage your existing customers to refer your startup to their friends, colleagues, or social networks. Incentivize referrals with rewards, discounts, or exclusive access to encourage word-of-mouth marketing.
- ❖ Partnerships and Collaborations: Identify strategic partnerships or collaborations with complementary businesses or influencers in your industry. Joint marketing efforts can help expand your reach and tap into new customer segments.

4. Measuring and Analyzing Results

Measuring and analyzing your marketing efforts is crucial to understand what's working and what needs improvement. Consider the following strategies:

- ❖ Key Performance Indicators (KPIs): Define relevant KPIs that align with your marketing goals. Examples include website traffic, conversion rates, customer acquisition costs, social media engagement, and customer lifetime value.
- ❖ Analytics Tools: Utilize web analytics tools, such as Google Analytics, to track and analyze website performance, user behavior, and conversion funnels. Leverage social media analytics and email marketing metrics to gain insights into engagement and campaign effectiveness.
- ❖ A/B Testing: Experiment with different marketing strategies, messages, or design elements using A/B testing. Compare the performance of different variations to optimize your marketing campaigns and improve results.
- ❖ Customer Feedback and Surveys: Regularly collect customer feedback through surveys, feedback forms, or customer interviews. Gain insights into customer satisfaction, preferences, and areas for improvement to refine your marketing strategies.

Effective marketing strategies play a vital role in the success of startups. By defining your brand identity, leveraging digital marketing channels, implementing customer acquisition strategies, and measuring results, you can establish a strong market presence and attract customers. Remember that the information provided in this section is a general overview and should not be considered professional advice. It is recommended to conduct further research and consult with marketing professionals to customize these strategies to your specific startup and industry. By implementing targeted and data-driven marketing strategies, you can position your startup for growth, increase brand awareness, and ultimately achieve your entrepreneurial dreams as an entrepreneur.

Leveraging Social Media and Content Marketing

Social media and content marketing have become integral components of a successful entrepreneurial journey. How startups can leverage social media platforms and content marketing strategies to build brand awareness, engage with their target audience, and drive business growth. From creating compelling content to selecting the right social media channels, this chapter provides actionable insights and best practices to help entrepreneurs effectively leverage social media and content marketing to achieve their entrepreneurial dreams.

1. Understanding Social Media Platforms

To effectively leverage social media for your startup, it's crucial to understand the different platforms available and their unique characteristics. Consider the following insights:

- ❖ Facebook: With billions of users, Facebook offers a robust platform for startups to reach a wide audience. Create a business page, share engaging content, and utilize Facebook Ads to target specific demographics and interests.
- ❖ Instagram: Known for its visual appeal, Instagram is ideal for startups with visually appealing products or services. Utilize high-quality images, videos, and stories to showcase your brand and engage with your audience.
- ❖ Twitter: Twitter provides a fast-paced, real-time environment for startups to share updates, and industry news, and engage in conversations with their audience. Utilize hashtags, retweets, and replies to expand your reach and build relationships.
- ❖ LinkedIn: LinkedIn is a professional networking platform that offers opportunities for startups to connect with industry professionals, share thought leadership content, and establish credibility within their niche.

2. Creating Compelling Content

Content marketing plays a pivotal role in building brand authority and engaging with your target audience. Consider the following strategies:

- ❖ Identify Your Target Audience: Understand your target audience's demographics, interests, pain points, and aspirations. Tailor your content to address their specific needs and provide value.
- ❖ Develop a Content Strategy: Define the goals and objectives of your content marketing efforts. Plan the types of content you will create (e.g., blog posts, videos, infographics) and establish a consistent publishing schedule.
- ❖ Engaging Blog Posts: Craft informative and engaging blog posts that address your audience's pain points, answer their questions, and provide actionable insights. Optimize your blog posts for search engines to increase organic traffic.
- ❖ Visual Content: Incorporate visual elements such as images, videos, and infographics into your content strategy. Visual content tends to capture attention and can be highly shareable on social media platforms.

3. Utilizing Social Media for Brand Awareness

Social media platforms offer vast opportunities for startups to increase brand awareness and reach a wider audience. Consider the following strategies:

- ❖ Consistent Branding: Maintain consistent branding across all social media platforms. Use your brand logo, colors, and tone of voice to create a cohesive brand identity that resonates with your audience.
- ❖ Engage with Your Audience: Actively engage with your audience by responding to comments, messages, and mentions. Encourage conversations, ask questions, and show genuine interest in your followers.
- ❖ Hashtag Campaigns: Create and leverage unique hashtags that align with your brand and resonate with your target audience. Encourage user-generated content and participation to increase brand visibility and engagement.

❖ Influencer Collaborations: Partner with relevant influencers in your industry to tap into their audience and expand your reach. Collaborate on content, giveaways, or sponsored posts to leverage their influence and credibility.

4. **Measuring and Analyzing Results**

Measuring and analyzing the effectiveness of your social media and content marketing efforts allows you to refine your strategies and optimize performance. Consider the following approaches:

❖ Social Media Analytics: Utilize built-in analytics tools provided by social media platforms to track key metrics such as reach, engagement, follower growth, and post-performance. Analyze these metrics to identify trends and adjust your content strategy.

❖ Website Analytics: Install tools like Google Analytics to track website traffic, referral sources, and user behavior. Identify which social media channels are driving the most valuable traffic and optimize your efforts accordingly.

❖ Content Performance: Monitor the performance of your content marketing efforts by tracking metrics such as page views, time on page, shares, and conversions. Use this data to identify top-performing content and areas for improvement.

❖ A/B Testing: Experiment with different content formats, headlines, visuals, or posting times using A/B testing. Compare the performance of different variations to optimize your content strategy and maximize engagement.

Leveraging social media and content marketing is crucial for entrepreneurs aiming to create brand awareness, engage with their target audience, and drive business growth. By understanding social media platforms, creating compelling content, utilizing social media for brand awareness, and measuring results, startups can establish a strong online presence and effectively communicate their value proposition. Remember that the information provided in this section is a general overview and should not be considered professional advice. It is recommended to conduct further research and adapt these strategies to your specific startup and industry. By implementing targeted and well-executed social media and content marketing strategies, entrepreneurs can unlock the potential of these powerful tools and pave the way for achieving their entrepreneurial dreams.

Sales Techniques and Customer Acquisition

In the journey of becoming an entrepreneur, mastering effective sales techniques and customer acquisition strategies is crucial. Some various approaches that startups can employ to drive sales, acquire customers, and fuel business growth. From understanding the sales process to building customer relationships and optimizing conversions, the actionable insights and best practices to help entrepreneurs excel in sales and customer acquisition.

1. **Understanding the Sales Process**

To effectively drive sales, startups must have a solid understanding of the sales process and the steps involved. Consider the following insights:

- ❖ Prospecting: Identify and target potential customers who are likely to be interested in your product or service. Utilize market research, customer personas, and lead-generation strategies to build a prospect list.
- ❖ Qualification: Assess the suitability of prospects by determining if they have a genuine need for your offering, the authority to make purchasing decisions, and the resources to invest in your product or service.
- ❖ Needs Analysis: Engage with prospects to understand their specific pain points, challenges, and goals. Conduct a thorough needs analysis to determine how your offering addresses their needs and provides value.
- ❖ Presenting Solutions: Position your product or service as the ideal solution to your prospects' challenges. Clearly articulate the benefits and unique selling points, and address any objections or concerns they may have.
- ❖ Closing the Sale: Guide prospects through the final steps of the purchasing process, addressing any remaining objections, and gaining commitment. Use effective closing techniques to secure the sale and move forward with the customer.

2. **Building Customer Relationships**

Establishing strong relationships with customers is essential for long-term success. Consider the following strategies:

- ❖ Active Listening: Practice active listening during sales conversations to understand your customers' needs, preferences, and concerns. Demonstrate empathy and show genuine interest in their success.
- ❖ Building Trust: Build trust by consistently delivering on your promises, providing exceptional customer service, and being transparent in your communication. Develop a reputation as a trusted advisor and reliable partner.
- ❖ Relationship Nurturing: Maintain regular communication with your customers. Provide ongoing support, share relevant industry insights, and offer value-added resources to strengthen the relationship over time.
- ❖ Customer Feedback: Encourage customer feedback and actively seek their opinions on your product or service. Use their feedback to make improvements, address any issues, and enhance the customer experience.

3. **Optimizing Conversions**

Optimizing your conversion process helps maximize the number of prospects who become paying customers. Consider the following strategies:

- ❖ Streamlined Sales Funnel: Design a streamlined and intuitive sales funnel that guides prospects through the purchasing process smoothly. Eliminate any unnecessary steps or barriers that may hinder conversions.
- ❖ Compelling Value Proposition: Clearly articulate the unique value proposition of your offering and how it solves your customers' pain points. Highlight the benefits and outcomes they can expect from using your product or service.
- ❖ Effective Sales Collateral: Develop high-quality sales collateral, such as brochures, presentations, or case studies, that effectively communicate the value of your offering. Provide compelling visual and written content to support your sales efforts.
- ❖ Follow-Up and Lead Nurturing: Implement a robust follow-up and lead nurturing system to stay engaged with prospects who are not yet ready to make

a purchase. Utilize email marketing, personalized messages, and targeted content to nurture leads and move them closer to conversion.

4. Customer Acquisition Strategies

Acquiring new customers is a critical objective for startups. Consider the following customer acquisition strategies:

- ❖ Referral Programs: Encourage existing customers to refer your product or service to their network. Provide incentives, such as discounts or rewards, for successful referrals. Leverage the power of word-of-mouth marketing.
- ❖ Strategic Partnerships: Identify strategic partnerships with complementary businesses or influencers in your industry. Collaborate on joint marketing initiatives, co-branded campaigns, or cross-promotions to tap into new customer segments.
- ❖ Targeted Advertising: Utilize targeted advertising channels such as search engine marketing (SEM), social media advertising, or display advertising to reach a specific audience segment. Develop compelling ad creatives and optimize your campaigns for maximum ROI.
- ❖ Content Marketing: Create valuable and informative content that addresses your target audience's pain points. Publish blog posts, videos, or podcasts that position your startup as a trusted resource and attract potential customers.

Mastering sales techniques and customer acquisition strategies is vital for entrepreneurs aiming to grow their enterprises and achieve their entrepreneurial dreams. By understanding the sales process, building strong customer relationships, optimizing conversions, and implementing effective customer acquisition strategies, startups can drive sales and acquire new customers. Remember that the information provided in this section is a general overview and should not be considered professional advice. It is recommended to conduct further research and adapt these strategies to your specific startup and industry. By implementing targeted and customer-centric sales and customer acquisition strategies, entrepreneurs can create a solid foundation for sustainable business growth. The key lies in consistently providing value, building trust, and fostering meaningful relationships with customers. By continuously refining and improving their sales techniques and customer acquisition efforts, entrepreneurs can position themselves for long-term success in the entrepreneurial landscape.

Building Customer Relationships and Loyalty

Building strong customer relationships and fostering loyalty are integral to the success of any entrepreneurial venture. Some of the strategies and practices that entrepreneurs can employ to establish meaningful connections with their customers, cultivate loyalty, and create a solid foundation for long-term business growth. From personalized communication to exceptional customer service, this chapter provides actionable insights and best practices to help entrepreneurs excel in building customer relationships and fostering loyalty.

1. **Understanding the Importance of Customer Relationships**

Strong customer relationships form the backbone of a successful enterprise. Consider the following insights:

- ❖ Customer Retention: Building strong relationships with existing customers is more cost-effective than acquiring new customers. Loyal customers not only make repeat purchases but also act as brand advocates, referring others to your business.
- ❖ Brand Advocacy: Satisfied customers who have a positive relationship with your brand are more likely to recommend your products or services to their friends, family, and colleagues. This word-of-mouth marketing can significantly impact your business's growth.
- ❖ Feedback and Improvement: Close relationships with customers provide valuable feedback that can be used to improve your products or services. Understanding their needs, pain points, and expectations allows you to tailor your offerings and enhance customer satisfaction.
- ❖ Competitive Advantage: Strong customer relationships can differentiate your business from competitors. When customers feel valued and connected to your brand, they are less likely to switch to alternative options solely based on price.

2. Personalized Communication

Personalized communication is key to building strong customer relationships. Consider the following strategies:

- ❖ Customer Segmentation: Divide your customer base into segments based on characteristics such as demographics, preferences, or purchasing behavior. This allows for targeted and personalized communication.
- ❖ Customized Messaging: Tailor your messaging to resonate with each customer segment. Use language and content that align with their interests, needs, and aspirations. Personalize emails, newsletters, and other communication channels.
- ❖ Relationship Building: Invest time and effort in getting to know your customers on an individual level. Engage in conversations, ask for feedback, and show genuine interest in their success. Building a personal connection fosters loyalty.
- ❖ CRM Systems: Utilize Customer Relationship Management (CRM) systems to store and manage customer data. CRM tools enable you to track interactions, preferences, and purchase history, facilitating more personalized communication.

3. Exceptional Customer Service

Providing exceptional customer service is crucial for building strong relationships and fostering loyalty. Consider the following strategies:

- ❖ Prompt Responsiveness: Respond to customer inquiries, concerns, and feedback promptly. Aim to exceed expectations by providing quick and helpful solutions to their problems.
- ❖ Empathy and Understanding: Show empathy and understanding when customers face challenges or issues. Listen actively, validate their concerns, and work collaboratively to find the best resolution.
- ❖ Consistency Across Channels: Deliver consistent customer service experiences across all channels, including phone, email, social media, and in-person interactions. This ensures a seamless and positive experience at every touchpoint.

- ❖ Employee Training: Invest in training your employees to deliver exceptional customer service. Equip them with the necessary skills, product knowledge, and problem-solving abilities to handle customer interactions effectively.

4. Loyalty Programs and Rewards

Implementing loyalty programs and rewards can incentivize customers to remain loyal to your brand. Consider the following strategies:

- ❖ Tiered Rewards: Create tiered loyalty programs that offer increasing benefits as customers reach higher levels. This encourages continued engagement and repeat purchases.
- ❖ Exclusive Offers: Provide exclusive discounts, promotions, or early access to new products or features for loyal customers. Make them feel valued and appreciated for their ongoing support.
- ❖ Personalized Rewards: Tailor rewards based on individual customer preferences and purchase history. This demonstrates that you understand and appreciate each customer's unique needs.
- ❖ Gamification: Introduce gamification elements into your loyalty program to make it more engaging and enjoyable. Incorporate challenges, competitions, and points systems that encourage customers to interact with your brand.

Building strong customer relationships and fostering loyalty are essential components of success for entrepreneurs. By understanding the importance of customer relationships, employing personalized communication, providing exceptional customer service, and implementing loyalty programs and rewards, entrepreneurs can create a loyal customer base and fuel business growth. Remember that the information provided in this section is a general overview and should not be considered professional advice.

It is recommended to conduct further research and adapt these strategies to your specific startup and industry. By prioritizing customer relationships and consistently delivering exceptional experiences, entrepreneurs can establish a competitive advantage and cultivate brand advocates who contribute to long-term success. By focusing on building meaningful connections and fostering loyalty, entrepreneurs can create a solid foundation for sustainable growth and live their entrepreneurial dreams.

Data-Driven Marketing and Analytics

In today's digital age, data-driven marketing and analytics have become fundamental to the success of entrepreneurial ventures. The power of data in driving marketing strategies, optimizing campaigns, and making informed business decisions. From gathering and analyzing data to leveraging insights for targeted marketing, the actionable guidance and best practices to help entrepreneurs harness the potential of data-driven marketing and analytics.

1. **The Role of Data in Marketing**

Data plays a pivotal role in shaping effective marketing strategies. Consider the following insights:

- ❖ Customer Insights: Data allows entrepreneurs to gain a deeper understanding of their target audience. By collecting and analyzing customer data, such as demographics, preferences, and behaviors, entrepreneurs can tailor their marketing efforts to resonate with their audience.
- ❖ Market Trends: Data-driven marketing enables entrepreneurs to stay informed about market trends, industry shifts, and competitive landscapes. By monitoring and analyzing market data, entrepreneurs can make proactive decisions and adapt their strategies accordingly.
- ❖ Campaign Optimization: Data provides valuable insights into the performance of marketing campaigns. By tracking key metrics, such as conversion rates, click-through rates, and engagement levels, entrepreneurs can optimize their campaigns for better results.
- ❖ Personalization: Data-driven marketing allows for personalized and targeted messaging. By leveraging customer data, entrepreneurs can create customized marketing campaigns that address the specific needs and interests of individual customers.

2. **Data Collection and Analysis**

Collecting and analyzing data is crucial for data-driven marketing. Consider the following strategies:

- ❖ Data Sources: Identify relevant data sources, such as customer interactions, website analytics, social media metrics, and market research reports. Utilize tools and technologies to collect and consolidate data from various sources.
- ❖ Key Metrics: Define key performance indicators (KPIs) that align with your marketing objectives. These metrics could include conversion rates, customer acquisition costs, customer lifetime value, and return on investment (ROI).
- ❖ Data Analysis Tools: Utilize data analysis tools and platforms to process and interpret collected data. These tools can provide visualizations, dashboards, and reports that help identify patterns, trends, and actionable insights.
- ❖ A/B Testing: Implement A/B testing methodologies to compare the performance of different marketing strategies or creative elements. This allows entrepreneurs to make data-driven decisions based on measurable results.

3. **Targeted Marketing and Personalization**

Data-driven marketing enables entrepreneurs to deliver targeted and personalized experiences to their customers. Consider the following strategies:

- ❖ Segmentation: Segment your customer base based on relevant criteria such as demographics, preferences, or purchase history. This allows for more targeted messaging and customized marketing campaigns.
- ❖ Behavioral Tracking: Use data to track customer behaviors and interactions across various touchpoints. This information can be leveraged to deliver personalized recommendations, relevant content, and tailored offers.
- ❖ Marketing Automation: Implement marketing automation tools and workflows to deliver personalized messages at different stages of the customer journey. Automation allows for timely and relevant communication based on customer actions or triggers.

❖ Dynamic Content: Utilize dynamic content that adjusts based on customer data, such as location, preferences, or past interactions. This ensures that each customer receives a tailored experience, increasing engagement and conversion rates.

4. Measuring and Optimizing Marketing Performance

Data-driven marketing empowers entrepreneurs to measure and optimize their marketing performance. Consider the following strategies:

❖ Performance Metrics: Define and track relevant performance metrics to evaluate the success of marketing campaigns. These metrics can include conversion rates, customer acquisition costs, customer lifetime value, and ROI.

❖ Continuous Testing: Implement a culture of continuous testing and experimentation. Test different marketing strategies, channels, messaging, and creative elements to identify what resonates best with your target audience.

❖ Iterative Optimization: Use data insights to make iterative improvements to your marketing efforts. Identify areas of underperformance, adjust your strategies, and test again to achieve better results over time.

❖ Attribution Modeling: Implement attribution models to determine the contribution of different marketing channels or touchpoints to conversions. This helps allocate marketing resources effectively and optimize budget allocation.

Data-driven marketing and analytics have revolutionized the way entrepreneurs approach marketing strategies and decision-making. By leveraging the power of data, entrepreneurs can gain valuable customer insights, optimize marketing campaigns, and deliver personalized experiences that resonate with their audience. Remember that the information provided in this section is a general overview and should not be considered professional advice. It is recommended to conduct further research and adapt these strategies to your specific startup and industry. By embracing data-driven marketing and analytics, entrepreneurs can make informed decisions, stay ahead of market trends, and achieve their entrepreneurial dreams. By utilizing data to inform marketing strategies, entrepreneurs can drive business growth, enhance customer experiences, and maximize their marketing ROI.

CHAPTER 4: SCALING YOUR ENTERPRISE

Operational Efficiency and Process Improvement

Operational efficiency and process improvement are critical components of building a successful entrepreneurial venture. The strategies and techniques that entrepreneurs can employ to streamline operations, optimize workflows, and enhance productivity. From identifying bottlenecks to implementing automation and continuous improvement methodologies, this chapter provides actionable insights and best practices to help entrepreneurs achieve operational excellence and drive sustainable growth.

1. **The Importance of Operational Efficiency**

Operational efficiency is crucial for the success and scalability of any enterprise. Consider the following insights:

- ❖ Cost Reduction: Improving operational efficiency helps reduce costs by eliminating waste, optimizing resource allocation, and increasing productivity. This allows entrepreneurs to allocate resources to growth initiatives and invest in innovation.
- ❖ Enhanced Customer Experience: Efficient processes enable entrepreneurs to deliver a seamless and positive customer experience. Streamlined operations result in faster response times, accurate order fulfillment, and improved service quality.
- ❖ Scalability and Growth: Operational efficiency lays the foundation for scalability. By optimizing processes and workflows, entrepreneurs can accommodate increased demand, expand their operations, and effectively manage growth.
- ❖ Competitive Advantage: Efficient operations give entrepreneurs a competitive edge. By delivering products or services more efficiently and effectively than competitors, entrepreneurs can attract and retain customers in a crowded marketplace.

2. Identifying and Analyzing Operational Processes

To improve operational efficiency, entrepreneurs must first identify and analyze their existing processes. Consider the following strategies:

- ❖ Process Mapping: Map out your existing processes to gain a visual understanding of workflows, inputs, outputs, and dependencies. This helps identify inefficiencies, bottlenecks, and areas for improvement.
- ❖ Value Stream Analysis: Conduct a value stream analysis to identify value-adding and non-value-adding activities in your processes. This analysis helps eliminate waste, streamline workflows, and improve overall process flow.
- ❖ Data Collection: Collect relevant data on process performance, such as cycle times, lead times, error rates, and customer feedback. This data serves as a baseline for measuring improvements and identifying areas of concern.
- ❖ Root Cause Analysis: Use root cause analysis techniques, such as the 5 Whys or fishbone diagrams, to identify the underlying causes of process inefficiencies or bottlenecks. This analysis helps target improvement efforts effectively.

3. Automation and Technology Integration

Automation and technology integration play a pivotal role in optimizing operational efficiency. Consider the following strategies:

- ❖ Process Automation: Identify repetitive and time-consuming tasks that can be automated. Implement software solutions, robotic process automation (RPA), or artificial intelligence (AI) technologies to streamline workflows and reduce manual effort.
- ❖ Integrated Systems: Integrate your various systems and software applications to facilitate seamless data flow and eliminate data silos. This integration improves collaboration, reduces errors, and enhances overall efficiency.
- ❖ Cloud Computing: Utilize cloud computing technologies to centralize data storage, access, and collaboration. Cloud-based solutions provide scalability, accessibility, and security, enabling entrepreneurs to focus on core business activities.

- ❖ Analytics and Reporting: Leverage data analytics tools to gain insights into operational performance. Implement dashboards and reporting mechanisms that provide real-time visibility into key performance indicators (KPIs) and facilitate data-driven decision-making.

4. **Continuous Improvement Methodologies**

Adopting continuous improvement methodologies is essential for sustained operational excellence. Consider the following strategies:

- ❖ Lean Principles: Embrace lean principles, such as just-in-time production, waste reduction, and continuous flow. Lean methodologies help eliminate waste, improve process efficiency, and enhance overall value delivery.
- ❖ Six Sigma: Implement Six Sigma methodologies to reduce process variation, defects, and errors. By utilizing statistical analysis and problem-solving techniques, entrepreneurs can achieve higher process quality and customer satisfaction.
- ❖ Kaizen Philosophy: Embrace the Kaizen philosophy of continuous improvement. Encourage employees to identify and suggest improvements, provide regular training, and foster a culture of innovation and learning.
- ❖ Agile Project Management: Apply agile project management principles to increase flexibility and responsiveness in your operations. Agile methodologies, such as Scrum or Kanban, enable entrepreneurs to adapt quickly to changing market demands and customer needs.

Operational efficiency and process improvement are pivotal for entrepreneurs striving to build sustainable and scalable enterprises. By prioritizing operational efficiency, entrepreneurs can reduce costs, enhance the customer experience, and gain a competitive advantage. Remember that the information provided in this section is a general overview and should not be considered professional advice. It is recommended to conduct further research and adapt these strategies to your specific startup and industry. By identifying and analyzing operational processes, integrating automation and technology, and embracing continuous improvement methodologies, entrepreneurs can streamline operations, drive productivity, and achieve operational excellence. By continuously striving for efficiency and process improvement, entrepreneurs can position themselves for growth, deliver exceptional customer experiences, and realize their entrepreneurial dreams. It is an ongoing journey that requires dedication, adaptability, and a commitment to continuous learning and improvement. By implementing the strategies outlined in this chapter, entrepreneurs can optimize their operational processes, drive efficiency, and create a solid foundation for long-term success.

Financial Planning and Funding Strategies

Financial planning and funding strategies are vital components of building a successful entrepreneurial venture. The importance of financial planning, and various funding options, and guide managing finances effectively. From creating a solid financial plan to securing funding for growth, this offers the actionable insights and best practices to help entrepreneurs navigate the financial landscape and achieve their entrepreneurial dreams.

1. The Role of Financial Planning

Financial planning is a critical aspect of entrepreneurial success. Consider the following insights:

- ❖ Goal Setting: Financial planning helps entrepreneurs set clear goals and objectives for their venture. By defining financial targets, entrepreneurs can create a roadmap for growth and measure their progress.
- ❖ Cash Flow Management: Effective financial planning enables entrepreneurs to manage cash flow efficiently. By forecasting income and expenses, entrepreneurs can ensure they have sufficient funds to cover operational costs and invest in growth initiatives.
- ❖ Risk Mitigation: Financial planning helps identify and mitigate potential risks. By assessing financial risks, such as market volatility or unexpected expenses, entrepreneurs can implement strategies to protect their business and ensure its long-term viability.

- Decision-making: Sound financial planning provides entrepreneurs with the necessary information to make informed decisions. By analyzing financial data and projections, entrepreneurs can evaluate opportunities, assess the viability of new initiatives, and allocate resources effectively.

2. **Creating a Financial Plan**

Developing a comprehensive financial plan is essential for entrepreneurs. Consider the following strategies:

- Budgeting: Create a detailed budget that outlines expected revenues and expenses. Identify fixed and variable costs, allocate resources to different areas of the business, and regularly monitor and adjust the budget as needed.
- Financial Projections: Develop financial projections based on market research, historical data, and industry benchmarks. Forecast revenues, expenses, and cash flow to assess the financial feasibility of your business plans.
- Risk Assessment: Conduct a thorough risk assessment to identify potential financial risks and challenges. Consider factors such as market volatility, competition, regulatory changes, and operational risks. Develop contingency plans to mitigate these risks.
- Financial Monitoring: Implement systems and processes to monitor key financial metrics regularly. Track metrics such as revenue growth, gross margin, profitability, and working capital to assess the financial health of your venture.

3. **Funding Strategies**

Securing funding is often crucial for entrepreneurial growth and scaling. Consider the following funding options and strategies:

- Bootstrapping: Bootstrapping involves self-funding your venture using personal savings, credit cards, or revenue generated from early sales. Bootstrapping allows entrepreneurs to retain full control and ownership but may limit initial growth opportunities.
- Friends and Family: Seek funding from friends and family members who believe in your entrepreneurial vision. This can be in the form of loans or equity investments.

Maintain clear communication, set expectations, and formalize agreements to avoid potential conflicts.

- ❖ Angel Investors: Angel investors are individuals or groups who provide capital to early-stage ventures in exchange for equity. They often bring industry expertise, mentorship, and valuable networks to the table. Prepare a compelling business plan and pitch to attract angel investors.
- ❖ Venture Capital: Venture capital firms invest in startups with high growth potential. They often provide larger funding amounts in exchange for equity and actively participate in strategic decision-making. Develop a solid business plan and be prepared for due diligence and negotiations.
- ❖ Crowdfunding: Crowdfunding platforms allow entrepreneurs to raise funds from a large pool of individuals who contribute small amounts. Create an engaging campaign, showcase your product or idea, and offer attractive rewards or incentives to attract backers.
- ❖ Grants and Government Programs: Research grants and government programs that support entrepreneurial ventures. These can provide non-dilutive funding, mentoring, or access to resources. Explore available opportunities that align with your business objectives.

4. Financial Management and Reporting

Effectively managing finances and maintaining accurate financial records are crucial for entrepreneurs. Consider the following strategies:

- ❖ Accounting Systems: Implement accounting software or hire professionals to ensure accurate and up-to-date financial records. Use systems that automate bookkeeping, invoicing, and financial reporting processes.
- ❖ Financial Controls: Establish internal financial controls to safeguard assets, prevent fraud, and ensure compliance. Implement processes for expense approvals, financial reconciliations, and regular audits.
- ❖ Financial Reporting: Generate regular financial reports, including income statements, balance sheets, and cash flow statements. These reports provide insights into the financial performance of your venture and aid in decision-making.

❖ Financial Forecasting: Continuously update and refine financial forecasts based on actual performance and changing market conditions. Use forecasting to anticipate future cash flow needs, identify potential funding gaps, and make proactive financial decisions.

Financial planning and funding strategies play a vital role in the success and growth of entrepreneurial ventures. By creating a solid financial plan, entrepreneurs can effectively manage cash flow, mitigate risks, and make informed decisions. Exploring various funding options enables entrepreneurs to secure the necessary capital to fuel growth and scale their enterprises. Additionally, implementing sound financial management practices and maintaining accurate records ensure transparency and accountability.

It is important to note that the information provided in this section is a general overview and should not be considered professional financial advice. Each entrepreneur's financial situation and funding needs may vary, and it is recommended to consult with a qualified financial advisor or accountant to tailor strategies to your specific circumstances.

By prioritizing financial planning, exploring funding options strategically, and implementing robust financial management practices, entrepreneurs can navigate the financial landscape with confidence and increase their chances of realizing their entrepreneurial dreams. Remember, building a financially healthy and sustainable venture requires ongoing monitoring, adaptation, and a commitment to financial excellence.

Building and Leading a Team

Building and leading a high-performing team is crucial for the success of any entrepreneurial venture. The strategies and best practices that entrepreneurs can employ to attract top talent, foster a positive work culture, and effectively lead their team. From defining roles and responsibilities to promoting collaboration and providing effective feedback, this chapter provides actionable insights to help entrepreneurs build a strong and motivated team that drives business growth.

1. The Importance of Building a Strong Team

Building a strong team is essential for entrepreneurial success. Consider the following insights:

- ❖ Diverse Skill Sets: A well-rounded team brings together individuals with diverse skill sets and expertise. This diversity enables the team to tackle complex challenges, capitalize on different perspectives, and drive innovation.
- ❖ Complementary Roles: Each team member should have clearly defined roles and responsibilities that complement each other. This ensures efficient workflow, avoids duplication of efforts, and maximizes productivity.
- ❖ Collaboration and Synergy: A cohesive team fosters collaboration and synergy. When team members work well together, they can leverage each other's strengths, support one another, and accomplish more than they could individually.
- ❖ Employee Engagement: A strong team promotes employee engagement and satisfaction. When team members feel valued, supported, and empowered, they are more likely to be motivated, productive, and committed to the success of the venture.

2. Attracting and Hiring Top Talent

To build a strong team, entrepreneurs must attract and hire top talent. Consider the following strategies:

- ❖ Define Job Roles and Requirements: Clearly define the roles and responsibilities for each position in your venture. Identify the skills, qualifications, and experience necessary for success in each role.
- ❖ Employer Branding: Develop a compelling employer brand that showcases your venture's mission, values, and culture. Highlight the unique opportunities and benefits of working with your team to attract top talent.
- ❖ Effective Recruitment: Implement effective recruitment strategies, such as leveraging professional networks, utilizing online job boards, and partnering with recruitment agencies. Ensure a thorough and fair selection process to identify the best candidates.

- ❖ Cultural Fit: Assess candidates for cultural fit during the hiring process. Look for individuals who align with your venture's values and can contribute positively to the team dynamic.

3. **Fostering a Positive Work Culture**

A positive work culture is key to maintaining a motivated and engaged team. Consider the following strategies:

- ❖ Communicate Vision and Values: Communicate your venture's vision, mission, and values to your team. Ensure that everyone understands and embraces the shared purpose and direction of the venture.
- ❖ Encourage Collaboration: Foster a collaborative environment where team members are encouraged to share ideas, collaborate, and support one another. Create opportunities for cross-functional teamwork and knowledge sharing.
- ❖ Promote Work-Life Balance: Support work-life balance by providing flexible work arrangements, promoting wellness initiatives, and encouraging time off. Show that you value the well-being of your team members.
- ❖ Recognize and Reward Achievement: Acknowledge and appreciate the accomplishments and efforts of your team members. Implement a recognition and rewards program that celebrates achievements and motivates individuals to excel.

4. **Effective Team Leadership**

Effective team leadership is essential for maximizing team performance. Consider the following strategies:

- ❖ Lead by Example: Set a positive example for your team by demonstrating the values, work ethic, and professionalism you expect from them. Be a role model and inspire your team through your actions.
- ❖ Communication and Transparency: Foster open and transparent communication channels. Keep your team informed about the venture's progress, challenges, and decisions. Encourage two-way communication and actively listen to your team members' input.

- ❖ Provide Feedback and Development Opportunities: Regularly provide constructive feedback to help your team members grow and improve. Offer opportunities for professional development, training, and mentorship to support their career growth.
- ❖ Empowerment and Delegation: Delegate tasks and responsibilities to empower your team members. Provide them with the autonomy and authority to make decisions and take ownership of their work. Trust their capabilities and support them in their roles.

Building and leading a high-performing team is a critical aspect of entrepreneurial success. By attracting top talent, fostering a positive work culture, and providing effective leadership, entrepreneurs can create a motivated and engaged team that drives business growth. Remember that building a strong team is an ongoing process that requires continuous effort, communication, and adaptation. By implementing the strategies outlined in this chapter, entrepreneurs can build a cohesive and high-performing team that propels their venture toward success.

Expanding Your Product Line

Expanding your product line is a pivotal strategy for entrepreneurial growth and success. The importance of product line expansion, explore different approaches to diversification, and guide on effectively expanding your offerings. From identifying market opportunities to managing product development and marketing, the actionable insights and best practices to help entrepreneurs navigate the process of expanding their product line and driving business growth.

1. **The Significance of Product Line Expansion**

Expanding your product line presents numerous benefits and opportunities for entrepreneurial ventures. Consider the following insights:

- ❖ Market Growth: By introducing new products or variations, you can tap into additional market segments and target a broader customer base. This expands your reach and potential for revenue growth.

- ❖ **Competitive Advantage:** Offering a diverse range of products enhances your competitive advantage by providing customers with more options and meeting a wider array of their needs. It can differentiate your venture from competitors and attract new customers.
- ❖ **Customer Retention:** A diversified product line increases customer loyalty and retention. By offering complementary products, you can encourage repeat purchases and build long-lasting relationships with your customer base.
- ❖ **Revenue Stability:** A well-diversified product line can help mitigate the risks associated with relying on a single product. It provides revenue stability, as fluctuations in demand for one product can be offset by others.

2. **Identifying Market Opportunities**

Identifying market opportunities is a crucial step in expanding your product line strategically. Consider the following strategies:

- ❖ **Market Research:** Conduct thorough market research to identify customer needs, preferences, and emerging trends. Analyze market gaps and unmet demands that align with your venture's capabilities and resources.
- ❖ **Customer Feedback:** Gather feedback from existing customers to understand their pain points, desires, and suggestions for new products. Utilize surveys, focus groups, and social listening tools to capture valuable insights.
- ❖ **Competitive Analysis:** Study your competitors' product offerings and identify areas where you can differentiate and outperform them. Look for gaps in their product lines that you can fill with innovative solutions.
- ❖ **Industry Trends:** Stay updated on industry trends, technological advancements, and changing consumer behaviors. Anticipate future needs and align your product line expansion with emerging market demands.

3. Product Development and Launch

Effective product development and launch processes are essential for successful product line expansion. Consider the following strategies:

- ❖ Product Roadmap: Develop a clear product roadmap that outlines the timeline, resources, and milestones for product development and launch. Align it with your venture's overall growth strategy and prioritize opportunities based on market potential.
- ❖ Prototype and Testing: Create prototypes and conduct thorough testing to ensure the quality, functionality, and market fit of your new products. Gather feedback from target customers and make necessary refinements.
- ❖ Scalable Production: Evaluate your production capabilities and ensure scalability to meet increased demand as you expand your product line. Establish reliable supply chains and manufacturing processes to support growth.
- ❖ Marketing and Promotion: Develop a comprehensive marketing and promotion plan to generate awareness and drive demand for your new products. Utilize a mix of online and offline marketing channels to reach your target audience effectively.

4. Managing Product Line Diversification

Managing a diversified product line requires effective planning and coordination. Consider the following strategies:

- ❖ Brand Cohesion: Maintain brand cohesion across your product line to create a consistent and recognizable brand identity. Ensure that new products align with your venture's values, positioning, and overall brand image.
- ❖ Pricing and Profitability: Develop pricing strategies that consider the cost of production, market demand, and competitive landscape. Evaluate the profitability of each product and adjust pricing as needed to maximize revenue.
- ❖ Inventory and Supply Chain Management: Implement robust inventory and supply chain management systems to optimize stock levels, minimize holding costs, and ensure timely delivery of products to customers.
- ❖ Customer Education and Support: Provide comprehensive customer education and support to guide customers in understanding and utilizing your expanded product line. Offer training materials, tutorials, and responsive customer service to enhance the overall customer experience.

Expanding your product line is a strategic endeavor that can fuel entrepreneurial growth and success. By identifying market opportunities, effectively managing product development, and implementing strong marketing strategies, entrepreneurs can diversify their offerings, attract new customers, and increase revenue streams. Remember that product line expansion requires careful planning, market research, and a customer-centric approach. By leveraging the insights and strategies outlined in this chapter, entrepreneurs can navigate the challenges of expanding their product line and position their venture for long-term success in a dynamic marketplace.

Strategic Partnerships and Alliances

Strategic partnerships and alliances play a vital role in the growth and success of entrepreneurial ventures. The significance of forming strategic partnerships, discuss the benefits they offer and provide guidance on how entrepreneurs can establish and leverage alliances to drive business growth. From identifying potential partners to negotiating and maintaining successful collaborations, the actionable insights and best practices to help entrepreneurs navigate the world of strategic partnerships and alliances.

1. **The Importance of Strategic Partnerships and Alliances**

Strategic partnerships and alliances offer numerous advantages and opportunities for entrepreneurial ventures. Consider the following insights:

- ❖ Access to Resources and Expertise: Forming partnerships allows ventures to gain access to resources, capabilities, and expertise they may not possess internally. This can include technology, distribution networks, market knowledge, or specialized skills.
- ❖ Market Expansion: Strategic partnerships can facilitate market expansion by leveraging the partner's existing customer base, distribution channels, or brand reputation. This provides opportunities to reach new markets and target a larger audience.

- ❖ Innovation and Collaboration: Collaborating with partners brings together diverse perspectives, knowledge, and ideas. This fosters innovation, encourages creative problem-solving, and enhances the development of new products or services.
- ❖ Risk Mitigation: Strategic partnerships can help mitigate risks associated with entering new markets, launching new products, or scaling operations. Sharing resources, costs, and risks with a trusted partner minimizes the burden on individual ventures.

2. Identifying Potential Partners

Identifying and selecting the right partners is crucial for successful strategic alliances. Consider the following strategies:

- ❖ Complementary Capabilities: Look for partners whose capabilities, expertise, or resources complement your venture's strengths and fill gaps in your value proposition. Seek partners with a shared vision and a compatible organizational culture.
- ❖ Market Alignment: Identify partners whose target markets align with yours. Look for opportunities to collaborate with ventures that serve similar customer segments or operate in related industries.
- ❖ Reputation and Trust: Evaluate potential partners based on their reputation, track record, and credibility in the industry. Choose partners who have a history of ethical business practices and a commitment to excellence.
- ❖ Networking and Referrals: Leverage your professional network, industry events, and referrals to identify potential partners. Engage in conversations, attend conferences, and actively participate in industry associations to expand your partnership opportunities.

3. **Negotiating and Establishing Alliances**

Negotiating and establishing successful alliances require careful planning and effective communication. Consider the following strategies:

- ❖ Clearly Define Objectives: Clearly articulate the objectives and expected outcomes of the alliance. Establish mutual goals and a shared vision to ensure alignment between the partnering ventures.
- ❖ Establish Mutual Benefits: Identify and communicate the benefits that each partner will gain from the alliance. This can include access to new markets, increased revenue streams, cost savings, or enhanced brand reputation.
- ❖ Legal and Financial Considerations: Work with legal professionals to draft comprehensive partnership agreements that outline the roles, responsibilities, and terms of the alliance. Consider financial arrangements, intellectual property rights, confidentiality, and dispute resolution mechanisms.
- ❖ Effective Communication Channels: Establish open and transparent communication channels between the partnering ventures. Regularly communicate progress, challenges, and updates to maintain alignment and build trust.

4. **Nurturing and Leveraging Strategic Alliances**

Nurturing and leveraging strategic alliances is essential for long-term success. Consider the following strategies:

- ❖ Relationship Building: Cultivate strong relationships with your alliance partners. Foster open lines of communication, establish trust, and invest in building personal connections to enhance collaboration and mutual support.
- ❖ Continuous Evaluation: Regularly evaluate the effectiveness and value of the alliance. Assess its impact on your venture's growth, market reach, and customer satisfaction. Make adjustments as needed to maximize the benefits.
- ❖ Collaboration Opportunities: Look for opportunities to collaborate beyond the initial alliance. Explore joint marketing initiatives, co-development of products or services, or shared research and development projects to further leverage the partnership.

- ❖ Exit Strategies and Contingency Plans: Develop exit strategies and contingency plans in case the alliance no longer aligns with your venture's goals or circumstances change. Ensure that there are mechanisms in place to protect your venture's interests if the alliance needs to be dissolved.

Strategic partnerships and alliances can be instrumental in driving the growth and success of entrepreneurial ventures. By identifying compatible partners, establishing effective collaborations, and nurturing long-term relationships, entrepreneurs can access valuable resources, expand their market reach, and foster innovation. Remember that building successful alliances requires careful planning, mutual benefit, and effective communication. By leveraging the insights and strategies outlined in this chapter, entrepreneurs can navigate the world of strategic partnerships and alliances to accelerate their entrepreneurial journey and achieve sustainable business growth.

International Expansion and New Markets

International expansion and entering new markets offer significant growth opportunities for entrepreneurs. The importance of expanding globally, the benefits of entering new markets, and guiding how entrepreneurs can navigate the complexities of international expansion. From market research and cultural considerations to strategic planning and risk management, the actionable insights and best practices to help entrepreneurs successfully expand their ventures into new markets.

1. **The Significance of International Expansion**

Expanding into international markets can bring numerous advantages and opportunities for entrepreneurial ventures. Consider the following insights:

- ❖ Access to Larger Customer Base: International expansion allows entrepreneurs to tap into larger customer bases and reach a broader audience. This can lead to increased sales, revenue growth, and enhanced brand recognition on a global scale.

- ❖ Diversification and Risk Mitigation: Entering new markets diversifies revenue streams and reduces dependence on a single market. This can help mitigate risks associated with economic downturns or market-specific challenges.
- ❖ Competitive Advantage: International expansion can provide a competitive advantage by offering unique products or services that are not readily available in the target market. Entrepreneurs can leverage their expertise and innovation to stand out in new markets.
- ❖ Learning and Innovation: Entering new markets exposes entrepreneurs to diverse cultures, consumer behaviors, and business practices. This foster learning, innovation, and the development of new ideas that can be brought back to the home market.

2. Market Research and Analysis

Thorough market research and analysis are essential for successful international expansion. Consider the following strategies:

- ❖ Market Selection: Identify target markets that align with your venture's products, capabilities, and growth objectives. Evaluate factors such as market size, growth potential, competitive landscape, regulatory environment, and cultural fit.
- ❖ Consumer Behavior and Preferences: Understand the target market's consumer behavior, preferences, and purchasing power. Conduct market surveys, analyze local trends, and gather insights to tailor your products or services to meet local demand.
- ❖ Competitive Landscape: Assess the competitive landscape in the target market. Identify key competitors, their market share, pricing strategies, distribution channels, and unique selling propositions. Determine how your venture can differentiate and compete effectively.
- ❖ Cultural Considerations: Study the cultural nuances, traditions, and social norms of the target market. Adapt your marketing messages, branding, and product positioning to resonate with the local culture. Pay attention to language, symbols, and customs to avoid cultural missteps.

3. **Strategic Planning and Execution**

Strategic planning and execution are crucial for a successful international expansion. Consider the following strategies:

- ❖ International Market Entry Strategy: Determine the most suitable market entry strategy based on your venture's resources, objectives, and risk tolerance. Options include exporting, licensing, joint ventures, franchising, or establishing wholly-owned subsidiaries.
- ❖ Legal and Regulatory Compliance: Familiarize yourself with the legal and regulatory requirements of the target market. Ensure compliance with local laws, intellectual property protection, product certifications, import/export regulations, and taxation.
- ❖ Supply Chain and Logistics: Establish efficient supply chain and logistics systems to support international operations. Ensure timely delivery, manage inventory, and establish relationships with reliable local suppliers and distributors.
- ❖ Localization and Adaptation: Customize your products, marketing campaigns, and customer experiences to suit the local market. Adapt packaging, pricing, product features, and promotional strategies to cater to the specific needs and preferences of the target market.

4. **Risk Management and Organizational Readiness**

Managing risks and preparing your organization for international expansion is vital. Consider the following strategies:

- ❖ Risk Assessment: Identify potential risks and challenges associated with international expansion. These can include political instability, currency fluctuations, legal disputes, cultural barriers, or supply chain disruptions. Develop risk mitigation strategies to minimize their impact.
- ❖ Financial Planning: Conduct thorough financial planning and ensure adequate capital to support international expansion. Consider factors such as market entry costs, currency exchange rates, working capital requirements, and potential fluctuations in revenue streams.

- ❖ Organizational Structure and Talent: Assess your venture's organizational structure and talent needs for international expansion. Determine whether additional resources, expertise, or local hires are required to support operations in the target market.
- ❖ Continuous Evaluation and Adaptation: Regularly evaluate the performance of your international expansion efforts. Monitor market dynamics, customer feedback, and key performance indicators. Adapt strategies and make necessary adjustments to optimize results.

International expansion and entering new markets offer exciting growth opportunities for entrepreneurs. By conducting thorough market research, strategically planning their entry, and effectively managing risks, entrepreneurs can successfully navigate the complexities of global expansion. Remember that each market is unique, and adapting to local preferences and cultural nuances is essential for success. By leveraging the insights and strategies outlined in this chapter, entrepreneurs can explore new horizons, expand their customer base, and unleash the full potential of their entrepreneurial ventures. International expansion opens doors to new opportunities, learning experiences, and the ability to make a global impact. With careful planning, a deep understanding of target markets, and a willingness to adapt, entrepreneurs can embark on a transformative journey towards growth, innovation, and living the entrepreneurial dream on a global scale.

CHAPTER 5: THE ENTREPRENEURIAL LIFESTYLE

Balancing Work and Personal Life

Achieving a healthy work-life balance is crucial for entrepreneurs to sustain their entrepreneurial journey and lead fulfilling lives. The importance of balancing work and personal life, exploring the challenges entrepreneurs face, and providing practical strategies to help entrepreneurs find harmony between their professional and personal commitments. From setting boundaries and prioritizing self-care to fostering supportive relationships and optimizing productivity, the valuable insights and actionable advice for entrepreneurs striving to create a balanced and meaningful life.

1. **Understanding the Importance of Work-Life Balance**

Work-life balance is essential for the overall well-being and long-term success of entrepreneurs. Consider the following insights:

- ❖ Well-being and Happiness: Achieving a balance between work and personal life promotes better physical and mental health, leading to increased happiness and overall life satisfaction.
- ❖ Sustainable Performance: Maintaining a healthy work-life balance helps prevent burnout and enables entrepreneurs to sustain high levels of performance and productivity in the long run.
- ❖ Relationships and Personal Fulfillment: Balancing work and personal life allows entrepreneurs to nurture meaningful relationships, spend quality time with loved ones, and engage in activities that bring them joy and personal fulfillment.

- Creativity and Innovation: Taking time for rest, relaxation, and personal interests fosters creativity, innovation, and fresh perspectives, which can positively impact entrepreneurial ventures.

2. Setting Boundaries and Prioritizing Self-Care

Setting clear boundaries and prioritizing self-care are key to maintaining a healthy work-life balance. Consider the following strategies:

- Establishing Work Hours: Define specific work hours and create a schedule that allows for dedicated time to focus on work-related tasks. Communicate these boundaries to clients, colleagues, and team members to manage expectations.
- Allocating Personal Time: Dedicate regular time slots for personal activities, hobbies, and self-care. Treat this time as non-negotiable and prioritize it as you would any other professional commitment.
- Unplugging from Technology: Set boundaries around technology use, such as designated times for checking emails or using social media. Establish tech-free zones or periods to disconnect and recharge.
- Practicing Self-Care: Prioritize self-care activities, such as exercise, meditation, adequate sleep, and healthy eating. Make self-care a non-negotiable part of your routine to ensure physical and mental well-being.

3. Optimizing Productivity and Time Management

Effective productivity and time management strategies can help entrepreneurs make the most of their work hours and create time for personal pursuits. Consider the following strategies:

- Prioritization and Focus: Identify the most important tasks or projects and prioritize them. Focus on high-value activities that align with your goals and delegate or eliminate tasks that don't contribute significantly to your success.
- Time Blocking: Divide your schedule into distinct blocks dedicated to specific tasks or types of work. Allocate time for focused work, meetings, strategic planning, and personal activities to maintain a balanced and structured approach to your day.

- ❖ Delegation and Outsourcing: Identify tasks that can be delegated or outsourced to free up your time for higher-value activities. Build a reliable team or network of professionals to assist with routine tasks or areas outside your expertise.
- ❖ Avoiding Multitasking: Multitasking can lead to reduced efficiency and increased stress. Instead, focus on one task at a time, giving it your full attention before moving on to the next.

4. **Fostering Supportive Relationships**

Nurturing relationships with loved ones, mentors, and a supportive community is essential for maintaining work-life balance. Consider the following strategies:

- ❖ Communicating with Loved Ones: Maintain open and honest communication with your family and loved ones about your work commitments, goals, and the need for support. Involve them in your entrepreneurial journey and find ways to create quality time together.
- ❖ Seeking Mentorship and Guidance: Connect with experienced entrepreneurs or mentors who have successfully achieved work-life balance. Seek their guidance and learn from their experiences to gain insights and practical tips.
- ❖ Building a Supportive Network: Surround yourself with like-minded entrepreneurs and individuals who understand the challenges and rewards of entrepreneurship. Engage in networking activities, join industry associations, and participate in entrepreneurial communities to find support and camaraderie.
- ❖ Collaboration and Delegating Responsibilities: Collaborate with trusted partners or colleagues to share the workload and responsibilities. Delegate tasks when appropriate, allowing others to contribute and grow within the venture.

5. **Reflection and Continuous Improvement**

Regular reflection and continuous improvement are essential for maintaining a healthy work-life balance. Consider the following strategies:

- ❖ Regularly Assessing Priorities: Reflect on your priorities and ensure they align with your values and long-term goals. Regularly assess whether your current commitments and activities contribute positively to your personal and professional life.
- ❖ Learning from Experiences: Reflect on past experiences and learn from them. Identify patterns of imbalance or areas where adjustments can be made to create a more harmonious work-life integration.
- ❖ Seeking Feedback: Seek feedback from trusted colleagues, mentors, or loved ones regarding your work-life balance. Listen to their perspectives and insights, and use them to make informed decisions and adjustments.
- ❖ dapting and Iterating: Recognize that work-life balance is a dynamic and evolving process. Be open to adapting and iterating your strategies as needed. Embrace flexibility and make adjustments when circumstances change or new opportunities arise.

Balancing work and personal life is an ongoing journey for entrepreneurs. By understanding the importance of work-life balance, setting boundaries, prioritizing self-care, optimizing productivity, fostering supportive relationships, and embracing continuous improvement, entrepreneurs can create a fulfilling and sustainable entrepreneurial lifestyle. Remember that work-life balance is unique to each individual, and there is no one-size-fits-all approach. It requires self-awareness, intentional choices, and a commitment to nurturing both professional and personal aspects of life. With dedication, resilience, and a balanced approach, entrepreneurs can thrive in their entrepreneurial endeavors while enjoying a meaningful and well-rounded life.

Maintaining Health and Wellness

Maintaining health and wellness is of paramount importance for entrepreneurs on their entrepreneurial journey. The significance of prioritizing physical and mental well-being delves into the challenges entrepreneurs face in maintaining a healthy lifestyle, and provides practical strategies to help entrepreneurs prioritize their health amidst their demanding entrepreneurial pursuits. From adopting healthy habits and managing stress to cultivating resilience and seeking support, the valuable insights and actionable advice for entrepreneurs striving to maintain optimal health and wellness while pursuing their entrepreneurial dreams.

1. **The Importance of Prioritizing Health and Wellness**

Prioritizing health and wellness is crucial for entrepreneurs to achieve sustainable success and lead fulfilling lives. Consider the following insights:

- ❖ Physical Well-being: Maintaining good physical health improves energy levels, enhances focus, and increases productivity – vital components for entrepreneurial success.
- ❖ Mental Well-being: Nurturing mental well-being helps entrepreneurs manage stress, make sound decisions, and foster creativity and innovation.
- ❖ Work-Life Integration: Prioritizing health ensures a harmonious work-life integration, enabling entrepreneurs to excel in both their professional and personal endeavors.
- ❖ Long-Term Success: By investing in their health and wellness, entrepreneurs improve their chances of long-term success and avoid burnout, which can derail their entrepreneurial journey.

2. **Adopting Healthy Habits**

Incorporating healthy habits into daily routines is essential for entrepreneurs. Consider the following strategies:

- ❖ Regular Exercise: Engage in regular physical activity that suits your preferences and fits your schedule. Physical exercise improves overall fitness, reduces stress, and boosts cognitive function.

- ❖ Balanced Nutrition: Prioritize a balanced diet consisting of nutritious whole foods. Fuel your body with the right nutrients to enhance energy levels, mental clarity, and overall well-being.
- ❖ Adequate Sleep: Prioritize sufficient sleep to rejuvenate your body and mind. Aim for a consistent sleep schedule and create a conducive sleep environment.
- ❖ Hydration: Stay adequately hydrated throughout the day. Carry a water bottle with you and make it a habit to drink water regularly.

3. Managing Stress Effectively

Entrepreneurship can be stressful, but entrepreneurs can adopt strategies to manage stress effectively. Consider the following approaches:

- ❖ Mindfulness and Meditation: Practice mindfulness and meditation to cultivate present-moment awareness and reduce stress. Dedicate a few minutes each day to quiet reflection and deep breathing exercises.
- ❖ Stress Management Techniques: Explore various stress management techniques such as deep relaxation, visualization, or engaging in activities that bring joy and relaxation.
- ❖ 3Time Management: Effectively manage your time to minimize stress. Prioritize tasks, set realistic deadlines, and delegate when necessary to avoid feeling overwhelmed.
- ❖ Work-Life Boundaries: Establish clear boundaries between work and personal life. Set aside specific times for rest, relaxation, and personal activities to recharge and rejuvenate.

4. Cultivating Resilience

Entrepreneurship often involves facing setbacks and challenges, but entrepreneurs can develop resilience to navigate these obstacles. Consider the following strategies:

- ❖ Embrace Failure as Learning Opportunities: View failures as valuable learning experiences rather than personal setbacks. Extract lessons, adjust your approach, and persevere.
- ❖ Develop a Growth Mindset: Adopt a growth mindset that embraces challenges and believes in continuous learning and improvement. Emphasize personal development and seek growth opportunities.
- ❖ Build a Supportive Network: Surround yourself with supportive individuals who can provide guidance, encouragement, and assistance during challenging times. Seek out mentors, join entrepreneurial communities, and network with like-minded individuals.
- ❖ Practice Self-Compassion: Be kind to yourself and practice self-compassion. Treat setbacks and challenges as part of the entrepreneurial journey and be patient with yourself as you navigate them.

5. **Seeking Support and Professional Help**

Entrepreneurs should not hesitate to seek support and professional help when needed. Consider the following approaches:

- ❖ Professional Networking: Engage in professional networking to connect with individuals who can offer guidance, advice, and resources related to health and wellness.
- ❖ Mentorship: Seek mentors who have successfully maintained health and wellness while building their entrepreneurial ventures. Learn from their experiences and seek their guidance.
- ❖ Professional Services: Consult health professionals, such as nutritionists, therapists, or fitness coaches, to receive personalized advice and support in maintaining optimal health.
- ❖ Accountability Partners: Find accountability partners who can help you stay committed to your health and wellness goals. Share your progress, challenges, and successes with them, and mutually support each other.

Maintaining health and wellness is a foundational pillar for entrepreneurs. By prioritizing physical and mental well-being, adopting healthy habits, effectively managing stress, cultivating resilience, and seeking support when needed, entrepreneurs can sustain their entrepreneurial journey while taking care of their overall health. Remember that health and wellness are ongoing commitments that require consistent effort and self-care. By investing in your well-being, you not only enhance your personal quality of life but also set the stage for long-term success in your entrepreneurial endeavors. Embrace the journey of maintaining health and wellness as an integral part of your entrepreneurial lifestyle, and enjoy the benefits of a balanced and thriving life.

Staying Motivated and Overcoming Challenges

Staying motivated and overcoming challenges are critical aspects of the entrepreneurial journey for entrepreneurs. The significance of maintaining motivation, exploring common challenges faced by entrepreneurs, and providing practical strategies to help entrepreneurs stay focused, resilient, and driven in the face of obstacles. From setting meaningful goals and embracing a positive mindset to utilizing effective problem-solving techniques and seeking support, the valuable insights and actionable advice for entrepreneurs striving to maintain motivation and overcome challenges on their path to entrepreneurial success.

1. **The Importance of Motivation**

Motivation fuels the drive and determination necessary for success in entrepreneurship. Consider the following insights:

- ❖ Sustained Focus: Motivation helps entrepreneurs maintain focus on their goals and vision, enabling them to persevere through obstacles and setbacks.
- ❖ Goal Achievement: Motivation provides the necessary energy and commitment to set and achieve ambitious goals, driving innovation and growth in the entrepreneurial journey.

- Resilience: Motivated individuals are more resilient, bouncing back from failures and setbacks with renewed determination and adaptability.
- Positive Mindset: Motivation fosters a positive mindset, enhancing creativity, problem-solving abilities, and the ability to inspire and lead others.

2. Setting Meaningful Goals

Setting meaningful and well-defined goals is crucial for maintaining motivation as an entrepreneur. Consider the following strategies:

- Vision and Purpose: Clearly define your vision and purpose as an entrepreneur. Understand why you are pursuing your entrepreneurial journey and how it aligns with your values and aspirations.
- SMART Goals: Set SMART (Specific, Measurable, Achievable, Relevant, Time-bound) goals that are challenging yet attainable. Break down larger goals into smaller, actionable steps.
- Goal Visualization: Visualize the successful accomplishment of your goals. Create a mental picture of the desired outcome and regularly revisit it to reinforce motivation.
- Milestone Celebrations: Celebrate milestones along the way to acknowledge progress and maintain motivation. Reward yourself for reaching significant milestones, reinforcing a sense of achievement.

3. Cultivating a Positive Mindset

A positive mindset is vital for staying motivated and overcoming challenges. Consider the following approaches:

- Positive Self-Talk: Practice positive self-talk and affirmations. Replace self-doubt and negative thoughts with empowering and encouraging statements.
- Gratitude Practice: Cultivate a gratitude practice by regularly acknowledging and appreciating the positive aspects of your entrepreneurial journey. Recognize the lessons learned from challenges and setbacks.

- ❖ Surrounding Yourself with Positivity: Surround yourself with positive influences, whether through supportive friends, mentors, or inspirational books and podcasts. Create an environment that fosters positivity and motivation.
- ❖ Embracing Failure as Growth: Reframe failures as opportunities for growth and learning. Embrace a mindset that views challenges as stepping stones toward success rather than insurmountable barriers.

4. **Effective Problem-Solving Techniques**

Entrepreneurship involves navigating various challenges, and entrepreneurs need effective problem-solving techniques to overcome them. Consider the following strategies:

- ❖ Analyze the Situation: When faced with a challenge, take a step back to analyze the situation objectively. Identify the root cause and potential solutions.
- ❖ Break it Down: Break down the challenge into smaller, manageable tasks. Focus on addressing each task individually, building momentum and confidence along the way.
- ❖ Seek Innovative Solutions: Encourage creativity in problem-solving. Explore alternative approaches, brainstorm ideas, and think outside the box to find innovative solutions.
- ❖ Learn from Others: Seek insights and advice from mentors, experts, or other successful entrepreneurs who have faced similar challenges. Learn from their experiences and apply relevant strategies to your situation.

5. **Seeking Support and Building a Network**

Entrepreneurs should not hesitate to seek support and build a network of like-minded individuals. Consider the following approaches:

- ❖ Entrepreneurial Communities: Join entrepreneurial communities or networks to connect with peers who understand the challenges of entrepreneurship. Share experiences, seek advice, and offer support to one another.

- ❖ Mentors and Coaches: Seek guidance from experienced mentors or coaches who can provide valuable insights and help you navigate challenges. Leverage their expertise and learn from their past experiences.
- ❖ Accountability Partners: Find accountability partners who share similar goals and values. Regularly communicate with them, set goals together, and hold each other accountable.
- ❖ Emotional Support: Surround yourself with a support system that includes friends, family, or support groups. Lean on them for emotional support during challenging times.

Staying motivated and overcoming challenges are integral to the entrepreneurial journey of entrepreneurs. By setting meaningful goals, cultivating a positive mindset, utilizing effective problem-solving techniques, and seeking support from mentors and like-minded individuals, entrepreneurs can maintain motivation and tackle obstacles with resilience and determination. Remember that motivation is not a constant state but a skill that can be nurtured and strengthened over time. Embrace the challenges, setbacks, and failures as opportunities for growth and learning, and let them fuel your ambition and determination to succeed. Stay focused on your vision, celebrate milestones along the way, and surround yourself with positivity and support. By staying motivated and developing effective strategies to overcome challenges, you can navigate the entrepreneurial journey with resilience, achieve your goals, and live the entrepreneurial dream.

Continuous Learning and Personal Development

Continuous learning and personal development are vital components of the entrepreneurial journey for entrepreneurs. The significance of ongoing learning, delve into the benefits of personal development and provide practical strategies to help entrepreneurs embrace a growth mindset, cultivate new skills, and foster self-improvement. From seeking knowledge and feedback to embracing challenges and nurturing curiosity, the valuable insights and actionable advice for entrepreneurs striving for continuous learning and personal growth on their path to entrepreneurial success.

1.　Embracing a Growth Mindset

Embracing a growth mindset is foundational to continuous learning and personal development. Consider the following insights:

- ❖ Openness to Learning: A growth mindset recognizes that abilities and intelligence can be developed through dedication and effort. It fosters a thirst for knowledge and a willingness to embrace new challenges.
- ❖ Embracing Failure as Learning: A growth mindset sees failure as an opportunity for growth and learning rather than a setback. It encourages resilience and the ability to extract lessons from setbacks.
- ❖ Belief in Potential: A growth mindset believes in the potential for improvement and development. It acknowledges that skills and abilities can be honed through practice and deliberate effort.
- ❖ Adaptability: A growth mindset embraces change and adapts to new circumstances. It encourages flexibility and the willingness to explore new ideas and approaches.

2.　Seeking Knowledge and Feedback

Entrepreneurs should actively seek knowledge and feedback to drive continuous learning and personal development. Consider the following strategies:

- ❖ Read Widely: Develop a habit of reading books, articles, and industry publications to broaden your knowledge base. Explore diverse topics related to entrepreneurship, leadership, personal development, and industry trends.
- ❖ Attend Conferences and Workshops: Participate in industry conferences, workshops, and seminars to learn from experts and gain insights into emerging trends and best practices.

- ❖ Engage in Online Learning: Take advantage of online learning platforms to access courses and educational resources that align with your entrepreneurial goals. Learn at your own pace and acquire new skills.
- ❖ Seek Feedback: Actively seek feedback from mentors, peers, and customers. Embrace constructive criticism as an opportunity for growth and improvement.

3. Cultivating New Skills

Cultivating new skills is essential for personal development and entrepreneurial success. Consider the following approaches:

- ❖ Identify Skill Gaps: Identify areas where you can improve your skills to enhance your entrepreneurial journey. Assess your strengths and weaknesses and prioritize skill development accordingly.
- ❖ Skill Development Strategies: Engage in deliberate practice and skill-building activities. This may include taking courses, attending workshops, seeking mentorship, or gaining hands-on experience.
- ❖ Continuous Improvement: Embrace a mindset of continuous improvement, consistently striving to enhance your existing skills and acquire new ones. Set aside dedicated time for skill development and practice regularly.
- ❖ Collaboration and Networking: Collaborate with individuals who possess complementary skills. Engaging in collaborative projects allows you to learn from others and broaden your skill set.

4. Nurturing Curiosity and Creativity

Nurturing curiosity and creativity enhance personal development and fuels innovation. Consider the following strategies:

- ❖ Embrace Challenges: Seek out challenges that push you outside your comfort zone. Embracing challenges stimulates creativity, problem-solving abilities, and personal growth.

- ❖ Explore New Perspectives: Foster a sense of curiosity by seeking out diverse perspectives and experiences. Engage in conversations with people from different backgrounds and industries to broaden your horizons.
- ❖ Engage in Creative Activities: Dedicate time to engage in creative activities that stimulate innovation and problem-solving. This could include brainstorming sessions, artistic endeavors, or exploring new hobbies.
- ❖ Reflect and Iterate: Regularly reflect on your experiences and learnings. Analyze what worked well and what could be improved. Use this self-reflection to iterate and refine your approaches and strategies.

5. Embracing Continuous Learning Culture

Creating a culture of continuous learning within your entrepreneurial venture is crucial for personal development and organizational growth. Consider the following approaches:

- ❖ Lead by Example: Demonstrate your commitment to continuous learning and personal development. Be open about your learning journey, share insights, and encourage others to embrace learning.
- ❖ Provide Learning Opportunities: Create an environment that encourages and supports learning. Provide access to educational resources, mentorship programs, and opportunities for skill development.
- ❖ Encourage Collaboration: Foster an atmosphere of collaboration and knowledge sharing. Encourage employees to share their expertise and learn from one another.
- ❖ Recognize and Reward Learning: Acknowledge and reward individuals who actively pursue learning and personal development. Celebrate achievements and emphasize the value of continuous learning within the organization.

Continuous learning and personal development are essential for entrepreneurs on their entrepreneurial journey. By embracing a growth mindset, seeking knowledge and feedback, cultivating new skills, nurturing curiosity and creativity, and establishing a culture of continuous learning, entrepreneurs can unlock their full potential and drive both personal and professional growth. Remember that learning is a lifelong journey, and there is always room for improvement and expansion of knowledge. Embrace challenges, be open to new ideas, and actively seek opportunities for growth and development. By prioritizing continuous learning and personal development, entrepreneurs can stay ahead of the curve, adapt to changing circumstances, and achieve their entrepreneurial dreams. Invest in yourself, foster a passion for learning, and let curiosity be your guide on the path to entrepreneurial success.

Giving Back and Social Responsibility

Giving back and social responsibility are integral aspects of the entrepreneurial journey for entrepreneurs. The significance of incorporating philanthropy and social responsibility into your business practices delves into the benefits of giving back to society and provides practical strategies for entrepreneurs to make a positive impact on their communities and the world. From adopting ethical business practices and supporting social causes to fostering employee engagement and sustainable initiatives, the valuable insights and actionable advice for entrepreneurs striving to create a business that not only achieves financial success but also contributes to the greater good.

1. **The Importance of Giving Back**

Giving back goes beyond financial contributions and encompasses making a positive impact on society. Consider the following insights:

- ❖ Social Impact: Giving back allows entrepreneurs to contribute to causes and organizations that align with their values, making a tangible difference in the lives of others.
- ❖ Brand Reputation: Incorporating philanthropy and social responsibility into your business practices enhances your brand reputation. Consumers are increasingly drawn to businesses that demonstrate a commitment to social causes.
- ❖ Employee Engagement: Engaging in philanthropy and social responsibility initiatives can boost employee morale and engagement. Employees are more likely to be motivated and fulfilled when they see their workplace making a positive impact.

- ❖ Creating a Better World: Giving back allows entrepreneurs to be a force for positive change, leaving a lasting legacy that extends beyond financial success.

2. Ethical Business Practices

Integrating ethical business practices is a crucial aspect of social responsibility for entrepreneurs. Consider the following strategies:

- ❖ Fairness and Transparency: Conduct business with fairness and transparency, ensuring that all stakeholders are treated equitably. Communicate openly with customers, employees, and partners.
- ❖ Environmental Responsibility: Adopt environmentally friendly practices within your operations. Reduce waste, conserve resources, and explore sustainable alternatives.
- ❖ Responsible Supply Chain: Ensure that your supply chain adheres to ethical standards. Partner with suppliers who prioritize fair labor practices and environmental sustainability.
- ❖ Corporate Governance: Establish strong corporate governance practices. Foster a culture of integrity, accountability, and adherence to legal and ethical standards.

3. Supporting Social Causes

Entrepreneurs can make a meaningful impact by supporting social causes that align with their values and business mission. Consider the following approaches:

- ❖ Community Engagement: Engage with local communities by actively participating in community initiatives, volunteering, or sponsoring local events. Understand the needs of the community and explore ways to address them.
- ❖ Strategic Partnerships: Collaborate with nonprofit organizations or social enterprises that align with your business values. Establish strategic partnerships to maximize your impact and leverage shared resources.
- ❖ Skills-Based Volunteering: Share your expertise by offering pro bono services or mentorship to nonprofits or entrepreneurs who can benefit from your knowledge and experience.Cause-Related Marketing: Develop cause-related marketing campaigns

that raise awareness and support for social causes. Connect your business objectives with the cause you champion.

4. **Employee Engagement and Empowerment**

Engaging and empowering employees in philanthropic initiatives can strengthen your social impact efforts. Consider the following strategies:

- ❖ Employee Volunteer Programs: Establish employee volunteer programs that provide opportunities for your team to contribute their time and skills to causes they care about. Offer paid volunteer days or organize group volunteer activities.
- ❖ Employee Donation Matching: Implement employee donation matching programs, where your business matches employee contributions to nonprofit organizations. This encourages employees to support causes they are passionate about.
- ❖ Social Impact Committees: Form employee-led social impact committees that guide philanthropic efforts within your organization. Involve employees in decision-making processes and empower them to drive social responsibility initiatives.
- ❖ Skills Development: Provide opportunities for employees to develop skills related to social impact and philanthropy. Offer training programs or workshops that educate employees on social issues and effective ways to make a difference.

5. **Sustainability and Environmental Stewardship**

Incorporating sustainability practices into your business operations demonstrates a commitment to environmental responsibility. Consider the following approaches:

- ❖ Energy Efficiency: Implement energy-efficient practices within your workplace. Invest in renewable energy sources, reduce energy consumption, and encourage employees to adopt sustainable habits.
- ❖ Waste Reduction and Recycling: Implement waste reduction strategies and establish recycling programs. Encourage employees to minimize waste and recycle materials.

- ❖ Sustainable Product Development: Consider the environmental impact of your products or services. Explore sustainable alternatives, source materials responsibly, and strive for eco-friendly manufacturing processes.
- ❖ Supply Chain Sustainability: Collaborate with suppliers who prioritize sustainability. Encourage environmentally responsible practices throughout your supply chain.

Giving back and social responsibility are essential components of the entrepreneurial journey for entrepreneurs. By incorporating ethical business practices, supporting social causes, engaging and empowering employees, and embracing sustainability, entrepreneurs can make a positive impact on their communities and the world. Remember that giving back is not just a philanthropic gesture; it is an opportunity to create a business that aligns with your values and contributes to the greater good. By prioritizing social responsibility, entrepreneurs can build a brand with a strong reputation, foster employee engagement, and leave a lasting legacy of positive change. Embrace the power of giving back, explore opportunities to support social causes, and integrate ethical and sustainable practices into your business. Together, we can create a world where entrepreneurship and social impact go hand in hand, making a difference that extends far beyond financial success.

Long-Term Vision and Legacy Building

Developing a long-term vision and building a lasting legacy are essential aspects of the entrepreneurial journey for entrepreneurs. The significance of having a clear vision for your business, delving into the benefits of legacy building, and providing practical strategies for entrepreneurs to create a sustainable and impactful business that leaves a lasting impression. From defining your purpose and values to developing a strategic roadmap and nurturing a culture of excellence, the valuable insights and actionable advice for entrepreneurs striving to build a business that transcends time and makes a meaningful difference in the world.

1. **The Power of a Long-Term Vision**

A long-term vision serves as a guiding force for entrepreneurs, providing direction and purpose. Consider the following insights:

- ❖ Clarity and Focus: A long-term vision helps you define your aspirations and sets the course for your business. It provides clarity and focus amidst challenges and uncertainties.
- ❖ Motivation and Inspiration: A compelling long-term vision fuels motivation and inspires you to overcome obstacles and pursue ambitious goals. It acts as a source of inspiration for yourself and others.
- ❖ Alignment and Decision Making: A well-defined vision aligns your actions and decisions with your desired outcomes. It serves as a reference point to evaluate opportunities and make strategic choices.
- ❖ Attracting Stakeholders: A compelling long-term vision attracts stakeholders, including employees, customers, and investors, who resonate with your purpose and want to be part of your journey.

2. **Defining Your Purpose and Values**

Building a long-term vision starts with defining your purpose and values. Consider the following strategies:

- ❖ Reflect on Your Why: Explore the underlying reasons for starting your entrepreneurial venture. Identify the core purpose that drives your passion and fuels your motivation.
- ❖ Define Your Values: Clarify the values that guide your business and personal life. Identify the principles and beliefs that are non-negotiable for you and integrate them into your organizational culture.
- ❖ Craft a Compelling Mission Statement: Develop a mission statement that encapsulates your purpose, values, and the impact you aim to create. Ensure it aligns with your long-term vision and resonates with stakeholders.

- Communicate Your Purpose and Values: Communicate your purpose and values to your team, customers, and other stakeholders. Consistently reinforce them through actions, messaging, and organizational practices.

3. **Developing a Strategic Roadmap**

A strategic roadmap outlines the path to realizing your long-term vision. Consider the following approaches:

- Set Clear Goals: Define specific, measurable, attainable, relevant, and time-bound (SMART) goals that align with your long-term vision. Break them down into actionable steps.
- Conduct Market Research: Gather insights about your target market, industry trends, and competitive landscape. Identify opportunities and challenges that may impact your strategic roadmap.
- Create a Business Plan: Develop a comprehensive business plan that outlines your strategies, marketing approaches, financial projections, and operational considerations. Continuously refine and adapt it as needed.
- Foster Agility and Adaptability: Remain open to feedback, market shifts, and emerging opportunities. Foster an agile mindset and be willing to adjust your strategic roadmap when necessary.

4. **Nurturing a Culture of Excellence**

Building a lasting legacy involves nurturing a culture of excellence within your organization. Consider the following strategies:

- Lead by Example: Demonstrate excellence in your work and behavior. Set high standards and be a role model for your team.
- Hire and Develop Top Talent: Surround yourself with talented individuals who share your values and align with your long-term vision. Invest in their growth and development through mentorship, training, and continuous learning.

- ❖ Encourage Innovation and Creativity: Foster an environment that encourages innovative thinking and creativity. Embrace new ideas, experimentation, and calculated risk-taking.
- ❖ Recognize and Reward Excellence: Celebrate and reward exceptional performance within your organization. Acknowledge individuals and teams that demonstrate excellence and contribute to the realization of your long-term vision.

5. Leaving a Lasting Legacy

Building a lasting legacy requires a focus on impact and sustainability. Consider the following approaches:

- ❖ Social and Environmental Responsibility: Integrate social and environmental responsibility into your business practices. Embrace sustainable initiatives, support social causes, and contribute to the well-being of your community and the planet.
- ❖ Mentorship and Knowledge Sharing: Pay it forward by mentoring aspiring entrepreneurs and sharing your knowledge and experiences. Help others achieve their goals and make a positive impact.
- ❖ Succession Planning: Develop a succession plan to ensure the continuity of your business and the preservation of your long-term vision. Identify and groom future leaders who can carry forward your legacy.
- ❖ Engage in Philanthropy: Give back to society by supporting charitable initiatives and organizations aligned with your values. Section: Conclusion

Developing a long-term vision and building a lasting legacy are crucial endeavors for entrepreneurs. By defining your purpose and values, creating a strategic roadmap, nurturing a culture of excellence, and embracing social responsibility, you can build a business that transcends time and leaves a positive impact on the world. A clear long-term vision provides direction, motivation, and focus, while well-defined values guide your decisions and actions. Developing a strategic roadmap helps you navigate the path toward your vision, adapt to market changes, and achieve your goals. Nurturing a culture of excellence ensures that your organization operates at its best, attracting top talent and fostering innovation. Finally, leaving a lasting legacy involves embracing social and environmental responsibility, engaging in mentorship and knowledge sharing, and planning for the future continuity of your business.

Remember that building a long-term vision and legacy is not a solitary endeavor. It requires the engagement and commitment of your team, stakeholders, and community. Communicate your vision, values, and goals clearly, and inspire others to join you in your journey. Through collaboration and shared efforts, entrepreneurs can create businesses that not only achieve financial success but also make a meaningful difference in the lives of people and the world.

Embrace the power of a long-term vision, take deliberate steps towards legacy building, and persistently work towards creating a business that leaves a positive and lasting impression. By doing so, you can become an entrepreneur who not only realizes their entrepreneurial dreams but also contributes to a better future for generations to come.

CONCLUSION

The Comprehensive Guide to Creating Products, Growing and Scaling Your Enterprise, and Living the Entrepreneurial Dream." Throughout this book, we have embarked on a transformative journey, exploring the multifaceted world of entrepreneurship and equipping you with the knowledge and tools to become a successful and impactful entrepreneur.

As an entrepreneur, you have learned that entrepreneurship is not merely about financial gains or personal fulfillment. It is about creating products and services that solve real-world problems, nurturing a thriving enterprise, and leaving a lasting legacy that transcends time. You understand that success is not measured solely by monetary achievements but by the positive impact you make on individuals, communities, and society as a whole.

In this concluding chapter, we delved into the critical aspects of long-term vision and legacy building. We discovered that a clear and compelling vision serves as a guiding force, providing direction and purpose to your entrepreneurial endeavors. Your vision acts as a beacon, leading you through challenges, inspiring you to overcome obstacles, and aligning your actions and decisions with your desired outcomes.

Building a legacy involves not only setting goals and achieving milestones but also nurturing a culture of excellence within your organization. By defining your purpose and values, you have created a strong foundation that guides your entrepreneurial journey. Your purpose and values act as a compass, ensuring that your decisions and actions are in alignment with your long-term vision. They shape your organizational culture and attract like-minded individuals who are passionate about your mission.

To transform your vision into reality, you have developed a strategic roadmap that outlines the steps needed to achieve your goals. This roadmap is a living document, adaptable to changing market conditions and emerging opportunities. By conducting thorough market research, crafting a comprehensive business plan, and fostering agility and adaptability, you are equipped to navigate the ever-evolving entrepreneurial landscape.

Throughout your journey, you have embraced the importance of nurturing a culture of excellence. By leading by example, hiring and developing top talent, encouraging innovation and creativity, and recognizing and rewarding exceptional performance, you have fostered an environment that promotes growth, collaboration, and continuous improvement. This culture of excellence ensures that your organization operates at its best, driving innovation and attracting individuals who are passionate about making a difference.

As an entrepreneur, you understand that your business is not an isolated entity but an integral part of society. You have embraced social and environmental responsibility, integrating sustainable practices into your operations, and actively contributing to the well-being of your community and the planet. By engaging in philanthropy, supporting charitable initiatives, and sharing your knowledge and experiences through mentorship, you are making a positive impact beyond your immediate sphere of influence.

Finally, you have recognized the importance of planning for the future and leaving a lasting legacy. By developing a succession plan, you ensure the continuity of your business and the preservation of your long-term vision. You are grooming future leaders who will carry forward your mission, values, and impact, ensuring that your entrepreneurial dream lives on.

Remember, the journey of an entrepreneur is not without its challenges. You may face setbacks, encounter unforeseen obstacles, and navigate through uncertain times. However, armed with the knowledge, strategies, and mindset presented in this book, you have the resilience and determination to overcome these hurdles and emerge stronger than ever.

As you embark on your entrepreneurial journey, keep in mind that success is not a destination but a continuous pursuit. Embrace a growth mindset, remain open to learning, and adapt to the ever-changing business landscape. Surround yourself with a supportive network of mentors, peers, and advisors who can provide guidance, inspiration, and accountability.

Above all, remember that success is not limited to individual achievements. It is about making a positive difference in the lives of others and leaving a lasting legacy. As an entrepreneur, you have the power to shape the future, create opportunities, and inspire change. Embrace the responsibility that comes with your entrepreneurial endeavors, and strive to build a business that not only thrives financially but also contributes to a better world.

Now, armed with the comprehensive knowledge and practical advice found in "Successpreneurs," go forth and unleash your entrepreneurial spirit. Dream big, take calculated risks, and persevere in the face of adversity. You have the power to create products, grow and scale your enterprise, and live the entrepreneurial dream. Embrace your journey as an entrepreneur and leave a lasting legacy that will inspire generations to come.

www.ingramcontent.com/pod-product-compliance
Lightning Source LLC
Chambersburg PA
CBHW082210220526
45470CB00010B/3109